GROUNDED & GROWING

Flourishing in Your Faith Journey

Bishop Tony McAfee

Grounded & Growing
2nd Edition

Copyright © 2025
Bishop Tony McAfee Ministries
151 Sycamore Place
Clinton, TN 37716
www.bishoptonymcafee.com

All rights reserved under International Copyright Law. Contents and/or cover may not be reproduced in whole or in part in any form without the express written consent of the publisher.

All Scriptures, quotations, unless otherwise indicated, are taken from the King James Version and New King James Version.

Scripture quotations taken from the (NASB®) New American Standard Bible®, Copyright © 1960, 1971, 1977, 1995, 2020 by The Lockman Foundation. Used by permission. All rights reserved. lockman.org

ISBN: 9798306616902
Imprint: Independently published

FOREWORD

"In a world that seems to be built on Jell-O, when nothing seems to be firm, Pastor Tony wants to plant a divine seed into your spirit that will solidify your foundations to withstand the shaking that permeates our world.

The old saying is true... if you stand for nothing.. you will fall for anything!

We need our homes, marriages, kids, grandkids, and everything temporal to be cradled in the strong arms of Faith and the Church!

We want 2025 to be the year of being grounded and growing like never before!

Fasten your seatbelts; we are taking back what has been stolen; it is our season... it's the GROUNDED and GROWING season!"
Philip Cameron, Founder of Orphans Hands.

"Do you have a goal of wanting to live with God forever? Have you ever wondered where to start? The longing you've had to get answers and results is over. This book will help keep you grounded and growing, maintaining faith in the Lord Jesus Christ.

A good foundation is the building block for anything standing the test of time. If you're ready to make a lifetime commitment, then this book is for you.

Ground and Growing's transformative principles have extended far beyond our local congregation, impacting global discipleship initiatives. Bishop Tony McAfee profoundly shared the book's core tenets throughout Tennessee's Church of God, establishing a firm foundation. This impactful curriculum subsequently flourished in churches across the Caribbean, enriching communities in Grenada, Trinidad, Tobago, Haiti, Zimbabwe, and South Africa."
Jim Black, Elder of Covenant Life Church.

"The strength and power of the Holy Spirit anoints faithful, humble servants to bring about his purposes for this kingdom of God.

I have had the privilege and honor of knowing and serving with Bishop Tony McAfee for 32 years, 26 of those years serving as his Armor Bearer. Bishop McAfee is an anointed, faithful, and humble servant of the Lord, who seeks to follow the leading and direction of the Holy Spirit.

In this book Grounded and Growing Bishop Tony McAfee has done an outstanding job of presenting firm foundational principals for Christians young or old, new, or seasoned in their faith and walk with God to learn how to become a more grounded and growing Christian. This book will encourage you and strengthen you to succeed in whatever purpose God has ordained for you in his kingdom."
Ray E Hagan Jr. Member and Elder Covenant Life Worship Center Clinton Tennessee

CONTENTS

Intro
Spirit-Filled Life — 5
Vision of the House — 7

Section 1.
Faith Foundations
1. God and His Word — 13
2. Repentance and Faith — 19
3. Water Baptism — 25
4. Holy Spirit Baptism — 29
5. Trinity of Giving — 36
6. Praise and Worship — 41
7. Fruit & Gifts of the Spirit — 46
8. Prophecy in the Church today — 52
9. Prayer & Fasting — 56
10. Communion and Divine Healing — 63

Section 2.
The Church
11. The Church — 68
12. Fellowship — 74
13. The Sheep and Shepherd — 79
14. Five-Fold Ministry — 84
15. The ministry of the Presbytery — 89
16. Women's Ministry in the Church — 93

Section 3.
Kingdom Living
17. Kingdom of God — 99
18. Resurrection of the Dead and Eternal Judgement — 102
19. Christian Home and Family — 107
20. Evangelism — 113
21. Possession — 118
22. Responsibility of Christian Citizenship — 122
23. Responsibility of Covenant Community — 126

Appendices
    Confirmation   129
    Covenant of Confirmation   131
    Personal Witness: Part 1   133
    Personal Witness: Part 2   140

Intro
SPIRIT-FILLED LIFE

Have You Made The Wonderful Discovery of The Spirit-Filled Life?

Every day can be an exciting adventure for the Christian who knows the reality of being filled with the Holy Spirit and who lives constantly, moment by moment, under His gracious direction.

The Bible tells us that there are three kinds of people:

Natural Man: One who has not received Christ.

"A natural man does not accept the things of the Spirit of God; for they are foolishness to him, and he cannot understand them, because they are spiritually appraised'

(I Corinthians 2:14, NASB)

Carnal Man: One who has received Christ, but who lives in defeat because he trusts in his own efforts to live the Christian Life.

"I, brethren, could not speak to you as to spiritual people but as to carnal, as to babes in Christ. I fed you with mil and not with solid food; for until now you were not able to receive it, and even now you are still not able; for you are still carnal. For when there are envy, strife, and divisions amongyou, are you not carnal and behaningn like mere, men?"

(I Corinthians 3:1-3, NASB)

Spiritual Man: One who is directed and empowered by the Holy spirit.

"He who is Spiritual appraises all things"

(I Corinthians 2:15, NASB)

Have you discovered the secret to a life of fulfillment and adventure? The answer lies in the power of the Holy Spirit and the choice to be led by Him. I once lived my life as a carnal man, struggling to find my way. I had accepted Christ, but I tried to live my Christian life through my own efforts, and I often felt defeated. It was only when I made the conscious decision to surrender my life to the Holy Spirit and be led by Him that everything changed.

I now wake up each morning with a sense of anticipation and excitement. Being filled with the Holy Spirit has transformed my life into an exhilarating journey. I am no longer bound by my own limitations but am empowered to live a life that glorifies God. This is the wonderful discovery I have made, and it is a choice that I must actively make each day. Choosing to be Spirit-led is an act of surrender and trust. It is recognizing that I cannot live the Christian life on my own and that I need the Holy Spirit's direction and empowerment. This choice is not a one-time decision but a moment-by-moment surrender, a continuous adventure of following His lead.

The Bible's promise of being directed and empowered by the Holy Spirit is a reality that I now experience. As I walk in step with Him, He guides my steps, and I am able to appraise all things with spiritual discernment. This is the adventure that awaits every believer who chooses to be led by the Spirit—an exciting and purposeful life, fully reliant on God's gracious direction. Will you join me on this adventure? It begins with the simple yet profound choice to be Spirit-led.

Intro
VISION OF THE CHURCH

This book, Grounded, and Growing, is a part of the vision that Pastor Cyndi and I received to train and equip believers in understanding the ministry of the local church (Ephesians 4:12).

The scriptures tell us, "Can two walk together, except they be agreed?" (Amos 3:3) We desire that as we study these principles found in God's Word, we will join together to do all God has planned and purposed for the church.

1. **HOW IS OUR CHURCH ORGANIZED?**

    1. PASTORS: Lead Pastors
        a. They feed and have oversight of God's flock.
        b. They give direction to the church as they hear from God.
        c. They preside as chairman at all church business meetings or appoint any church officer to preside over the meeting in the event of their absence.
        d. All business transactions or spending of the church funds must be reviewed by the pastors or by one appointed.

    2. PASTORAL STAFF:
        a. Assist the pastors in ministering to the church's needs in any area.
        b. Perform weddings and funeral services as the needs arise.
        c. Coordinate the pulpit activities in the absence of the pastors.

3. ELDERS
    a. Serve as an advisory board for the Pastor.
    b. Assist and support the pastoral staff.
    c. Support the overall program of the church by the following: Attending elder's meetings, praying for the sick as the word of God teaches in the book of James.
    d. An Elder, ministers to the needs of the congregation (such as encouraging parishioners by way of visitation, phone calls, and bereavement of a church member or their immediate family). They are generally called upon to make visit of the geographical region the deceased are from.
    e. An Elder, is to assist the pastor with leading sand observing the ordinances such as communion etc.
    f. Elders lead by example in the following ways: Being present for a minimum of 50% of church services; faithfully attending a focus group; tithing; following through on "Elder on call rotation".

4. OFFICERS: In addition to the officers mentioned above, you also have the Secretary, and Trustees:
    a. The Secretary is responsible for issuing notices for committee and church business meetings and keeps all meeting minutes for said meetings unless the Pastor directs an Elder to keep the minutes.
    b. In addition, the Secretary, along with the appointed Elder, shall receive and be entrusted with the finances and securities of the church. He/she keeps account of all monies and prepares a financial report issued by Chitwood and Chitwood (CPA Accountant) on a monthly basis and for Elders Meetings as needed. These

persons are responsible for keeping the Pastor abreast of church finances as well as, communicating the financial standing of the church tithe paying membership. The clerk prepares reports for the General Headquarters and State Office and accompanies them.
    c. Secretary prepares monthly report for General Headquarters and State Office and accompanies. (online)
    d. Trustee - two (2) or more: They attend to all legal business in connection with the property of the church as instructed by the pastor of the church and sanctioned by the fellowship. They sign all deeds or documents dealing with real estate of the church if need be. The trustees can be made up of a minimum of 1 layman and one elder or two responsible tithe paying mature laymen in the church body as recommended to board of elders by pastor. Trustees' tenure is generally a two-year term unless church board reappoints them for another two-year term.

5. Sweet Process
    a. The "Sweet Process" is an essential guide for our church. It serves as a means for maintaining order and efficiency in our daily operations. From reserving rooms for events to completing all necessary tasks, each step is clearly outlined, leaving no room for confusion or error. This manual is constantly updated to ensure that our church functions at its best. Not only does the "Sweet Process" help to keep things running smoothly, but it also serves as a valuable resource for all members of the church. By following the outlined procedures, we are able to maintain a

high level of organization and structure. This not only benefits our current members but also provides a solid foundation for future growth and expansion. The "Sweet Process" is an integral part of our church's daily operations. It is a testament to our dedication to excellence and our commitment to upholding the values and principles of our fellowship. With the support and guidance of our trustees, elders, and responsible laymen, we are able to keep our church functioning at its best, ensuring that all members and visitors have a positive and meaningful experience.

2. HOW DO WE ACCOMPLISH THE VISION OF THE HOUSE?

1. Build with balance: Matthew 16:18-19 - Jesus Christ is the Rock.
    a. John the Baptist: political reformer confronted the government of his day with a new message. The Kingdom of God is at Hand! The message of repentance.
    b. Elijah: Man of faith, miracles, and a prophet of the law and judgment.
    c. Jeremiah: Prophet weeping over the people. Desired to see God's people shepherded.

2. Use the building blocks God has placed in our hands:
    a. Both the written and spoken word.
    b. Exposure to the 5-fold ministry (Apostles, Prophets, etc.)
    c. Ministry sets the example.
    d. Spiritual authority.

3. WHAT IS THE "VISION OF THE HOUSE?"

The prophetic word has been instrumental in directing the steps of Pastors Cyndi, myself, and the congregation of Covenant Life Church. Areas of ministry are listed below that have been birthed in the hearts of our pastors to benefit the individual believer and the Body of Christ at large.

1. The Church is to be a **TRAINING CENTER**
    a. First Principles: covenant commitments, foundational fundamentals, fundamentals of faith.
    b. Ministry provided for persons from the womb to the tomb.

2. The Church is called to **REACH OUT TO EVERYONE**
    a. Television/Radio
    b. Missions
    c. Children
    d. Senior Citizens
    e. Youth
    f. Men's and Women's Fellowships
    g. Music Ministry
    h. Evangelism
    i. Focus Groups

3. The Church is called **POSITIVELY to AFFECT RELIGIOUS SOCIAL AND POLITICAL AREAS OF LIFE, BUILDING BRIDGES NOT WALLS.**
    a. Make Heaven Crowded Campaign
    b. Family Crusades
    c. National Disaster Relief
    d. The Run to The Son Car Show
    e. Encourage believers to be involved in the political process, Christian Coalition.

4. The Church is to build **CITY OF REFUGE**

5. The Church is to reproduce CHURCH **PLANTING**

FOUNDATIONS OF FAITH
GOD AND HIS WORD

Essential for our growth and development as Christians is an understanding of God's will through His Word (Ephesians 5:17). God desires that we know Him and has provided His Word to be a governing or guiding factor in our lives. 2 Timothy 3:16-17 says: "All scripture is given by inspiration of God, and is profitable for doctrine, for reproof, for correction, for instruction in righteousness: That the man of God may be perfect, thoroughly furnished unto all good works." God Himself is our source, strength, and sustenance (Acts 17:28).

1. WHAT IS THE NATURE OF GOD?

1. God is Spirit.
    a. God is not limited to or confined to a physical body or the dimensions of space or time (John 4:24).

2. God is perfect (Matthew 5:48).

3. God is personal.
    a. He is concerned with our needs and desires to make provision for His people (I Peter 5:6,7; Matthew 6:25-34).

2. WHAT ARE SOME OF THE ATTRIBUTES OF GOD?

1. He is eternal (Psalm 90:1,2; Rev. 1:8).

2. Immutable (Unchangeable) (Malachi 3:6).

3. Omnipotent (All-Powerful) (Jeremiah 32:17, Psalm 62:11).

4. Omniscient (All-Knowing) (Psalm 139:1-4).

5. Omnipresent (Everywhere) (Jeremiah 23:23,24).

6. Holy (Leviticus 11:44,45).

7. Righteous (God's holiness in action) (Romans 3:25,26).

8. Merciful (Exodus 34:6,7).

3. WHAT IS MEANT BY THE "TRIUNE NATURE OF GOD?"

1. In God, there are 3 Divine Identities revealed to man:
   a. Father
   b. Son
   c. Holy Spirit

2. These 3 Identities are revealed as follows:
   a. The Father - Work of Creation (Genesis 1:1).
   b. The Son - Work of Redemption (Galatians 4:4-6).
   c. The Holy Spirit - Work of Sanctification (I Peter 1:2).

3. In Jesus dwells the fullness of the Godhead bodily. (Col. 2:9) Together, these 3 work to Achieve God's Purposes on the Earth (John 1:1, Deuteronomy 6:4, I John 5:7,8).

4. WHAT IS THE RELATIONSHIP BETWEEN GOD AND THE BIBLE?

God's Word is the revelation of Jesus Christ to man (II Timothy 3:15, John 20:31, I John 5:13).

5. WHO IS THE AUTHOR OF THE WORD?

1. Holy Spirit

a. God used man as a vehicle to make known His revelation (2 Peter 1:21).
   b. David and Isaiah (authors of Old Testament Scripture) were prompted to speak by the Holy Ghost (Acts 1:16 and 28:25).

2. The Holy Ghost is the source of infallible revelation.
   a. God's Word is not devised by man's intellect (2 Timothy 3:16,17).
   b. It is not subject to private interpretations (2 Peter 1:20). The Word speaks. Man does not speak to the Word.

6. GOD'S WORD IS A SOURCE OF POWER

1. Dividing Power as a "sword" (Hebrews 4:12).

2. Reflecting Power as a "mirror" (James 1:22-25).

3. Cleansing Power as a "detergent" (Ephesians 5:26; John 15:3).

4. Reproductive Power, as a "seed" (I Peter 1:23)

5. Nourishing Power, as "food" (Milk of the Word - I Peter 1:19, 2:2).

6. Guiding Power, as a "lamp" (Psalm 119:105, II Peter 1:19).

7. Power of God unto salvation (Romans 1:16)

7. WHAT WILL READING THE WORD OF GOD DO FOR US?

When we receive His Word and appropriate it in our lives, it produces and shall prosper that which He sent it to (Isaiah 55:11).

1. Cleanse our ways (Psalm 119:9).

2. Produces Faith (Romans 10:17).

3. Begins a process of change, and our minds are renewed with God's thoughts and purposes for our lives (Psalm 19:7; Romans 12:2).

4. It brings peace that we can obtain in no other way (Isaiah 55:8-12; Philippians 4:7).

8. IS GOD'S WORD COMPLETE IN ITSELF?

God's Word, both the Old and the New Testament, is complete.

1. One shall not add to, nor diminish from, the Word of God (Deuteronomy 4:2, 12:32).

2. We are warned of the consequences of adding to or taking from God's Word (Revelation 22:18,19).

9. WHAT IS THE PURPOSE OF GOD GIVING US THE WORD?

1. It authenticates the divinity of Jesus Christ (John 20:31; 1st John 5:13).

2. It is an instruction manual for spiritual discernment and living a holy, successful life before God (2 Timothy 3:16,17).

a. Doctrine
   b. Reproof
   c. Correction
   d. Instruction in righteousness

The Word of God is a standard by which something can be judged right or wrong (Isaiah 8:19, 20). It was written for our learning (Romans 15:4) and our admonition, training us by both instruction and warning (I Corinthians 10:11). It is our responsibility to be a "doer" and not only a "hearer" of God's Word (James 1:22-25).

STUDY QUESTIONS

1. What is the nature of God?

_____
_____
_____
_____

2. What attributes belong to God?

_____
_____
_____
_____

3. What is the "trinity"?

_____
_____
_____
_____

4. Who is the author of the Bible?
_____
_____
_____

5. What will practicing the Word of God do in our lives?
_____
_____
_____
_____

6. What is God's purpose in giving us the Bible?
_____
_____
_____
_____

FOUNDATIONS OF FAITH
REPENTANCE AND FAITH

Repentance from dead works and faith in God are two foundational truths in Hebrews 6:1,2. Repentance is the first step in building a successful foundation in the believer's life, while faith in God is the essence of the entire Christian walk. God commands that man repent; there is no option or choice (Acts 17:30). Repentance and faith are gifts God gives us – we turn from our ways to follow His way. Likewise, repentance and faith go beyond our initial experience of salvation but work actively throughout our walk of sanctification. (Note: Sanctification is a walk).

1.   WHAT DOES REPENTANCE MEAN?

It means a "change of mind" or a change of heart and attitude. It means a radical change in one's attitude toward sin and God. It implies conscious moral separation and a personal decision to forsake sin and enter fellowship with God.

2.   WHAT IS THE IMPORTANCE OF REPENTANCE?

   1. Repentance is commanded by God (Acts 17:30).

   2. Essential for salvation (Mark 1:15).

   3. It is a gift from God (Acts 11:18; 2 Timothy 2:25).

   4. God desires it for all men (2 Peter 3:9).

3.   REPENTANCE CALLS FOR A RENUNCIATION OF SELF-CONFIDENCE AND WILL INITIATE CONFIDENCE IN GOD.

   1. Our way leads us astray (Isaiah 53:6).

2. We must confess, turn from sin, and place our confidence in God (Judge 10:15,16).
3. We must repent and turn toward God (Acts 26:19,20).

4. We must turn from our idols and serve God (I Thessalonians 1:8,9).

4. **WHAT DOES REPENTANCE PROVIDE FOR THE BELIEVER?**

JUSTIFICATION - or right standing with God.

1. Justification is a change in man's standing or relation before God. It is an act of God that frees penitent sinners from the guilt and penalty of sin.

2. To justify means to declare righteousness; when God justifies a man, he acquits him - not on the grounds of man's innocence, but of His own love and grace (Romans 3:20-26).

5. **WHY DO WE NEED JUSTIFICATION?**

1. Because man rebelled against God and entered sin, there is a separation between man and God. All men are natural sinners, condemned by a just, righteous, and Holy God (Romans 3:10-18,23).

2. Therefore, God must transfer our guilt onto His account. The death of Jesus made this transfer and forgiveness of sins possible (2 Corinthians 5:21).

6. **HOW DO WE RECEIVE JUSTIFICATION?**

1. By the grace of God (Romans 3:24; Titus 3:7).

2. Through the blood of Jesus Christ (Romans 5:9; Hebrews 9:22).

3. By faith (Romans 5:1,2; Galatians 2:16).

7. WHAT ARE THE RESULTS OF JUSTIFICATION?

1. Removal of the penalty of sin (Romans 4:7; II Corinthians 5:19).

2. Condemnation is gone (Romans 8:1, 33,34).

3. Peace with God (Ephesians 2:14-17).

4. Christ's righteousness is ours (Romans 4:5; II Corinthians 5:21).

8. WHAT IS FAITH?

Faith means belief, faithfulness, reliability, trust, confidence, firm persuasion, assurance, or strong conviction. "Now faith is the assurance (the confirmation, the title-deed) of the things we hope for, being proof of things we do not see and the conviction of their reality - faith perceiving as real fact what is not revealed to the senses." (Hebrews 11:1, AMP Version).

9. WHAT CAUSES FAITH TO ARISE IN OUR HEART?

The Word of God: "So then faith cometh by hearing and hearing by the Word of God" (Romans 10:17).

There are several ways that we can receive the Word of God:

1. The preaching of the Gospel (Titus 1:3; Romans 10:8; 1 Thessalonians 2:13).

2. Through the written Word (Luke 24:45; Psalm 119:105).

3. In times of prayer (2 Corinthians 12:8,9; Isaiah 65:24; Jeremiah 33:3).

4. A word of exhortation by another Christian (Colossians 3:16).

5. In dreams and/or visions (Acts 2:17).

6. The audible voice of God (Acts 9:4-6).

7. God speaks through His Word (I Samuel 3:21).

8. Angels (Daniel 10:11,12; Acts 27:23).

10. HOW IMPORTANT IS FAITH?

1. We are saved by faith (Ephesians 2:8; Romans 5:1).

2. The just shall live by faith (Hebrews 10:38).

3. Kept by faith (I Peter 1:5; I John 5:4).

4. We are healed by faith (James 5:15).

5. We cannot please God without faith (Hebrews 11:5,6).

6. We overcome difficulties by faith (Ephesians 6:16; I John 5:4).

FAITH

Proverbs 28:13 encourages the believer that he must not only confess his sins but forsake them. We cannot fully rely on the Lord as long as we trust our efforts. Repentance prepares us to believe, trust, or have faith in God. Faith is the key; it opens the door to pleasing our Lord; without faith, we can never become firmly established in the ways of God (Isaiah 7:9). Our attempts toward making ourselves acceptable to God are futile. God must turn our hearts from self-confidence and birth within us a desire to serve the living God (Hebrews 9:14).

STUDY QUESTIONS

1. What is the meaning of repentance?

_____
_____
_____
_____

2. Why is repentance important?

_____
_____
_____
_____

3. What is justification?

_____
_____
_____
_____

4. How do we become justified?

5. What are the results of justification?

6. What is faith?

7. Why is faith so important?

FOUNDATIONS OF FAITH
WATER BAPTISM

Water Baptism in the New Testament signifies that you died with Christ on the cross, were buried with Him, and were risen with Him to New Life.

According to scripture, water baptism is not a matter of choice but a command. Water Baptism is more than a mere ritual of ceremony. Its meaning always includes the entire redemptive work of the Lord Jesus Christ. (Acts 2:38)

1. BAPTISM MEANS COMPLETELY IMMERSED OR SUBMERGED UNDER WATER.

2. WHAT ARE THE REQUIREMENTS FOR BAPTISM?

1. Hearing and obeying God's Word (Acts 2:41; John 14:15; Acts 16:14).

2. Conviction of sin (Acts 2:27-39).

3. Repentance (Acts 2:38).

4. Faith (Mark 16:16; Acts 8:12, 36, 37).

3. WHAT HAPPENS TO THE BELIEVER IN WATER BAPTISM?

In Water Baptism, there is a definite inward work within the believer's heart. The Holy Spirit performs a spiritual operation known as circumcision.

1. Circumcision in the Old Testament was a command (Genesis 17:10). It foreshadowed the circumcision of the heart.

a. Sign and seal of covenant relationship with God and Abraham (Genesis 17:11).
  b. Marked the Israelites as God's chosen people and set them apart as His personal property (Genesis 17:13).
2. Their relationship was maintained with God through their obedience to His command of circumcision.

3. Circumcision, not only of their foreskin but also of their hearts (Deuteronomy 30:5,6; 10:16,17).

4. Circumcision of the heart - as circumcision of the foreskin was a token or sign of the Old Covenant (Genesis 17:11), water baptism is the circumcision of the New Covenant. The true sign of the New Covenant believer is a circumcised heart. Our "old nature" or "body of sin" is cut away with all its desires and lusts.
  a. Must have a circumcised heart (Romans 2:28,29).
  b. The New Covenant declares in Hebrews 8:6-10:
    i. The Lord is our God.
    ii. We are His people.

4. WHAT IS THE MEANING OF WATER BAPTISM?

We are baptized into the name of the Father, the Son, and the Holy Spirit (Matthew 28:19).

1. What is the Father's name?
   a. The Lord (Exodus 3:15).
   b. The Lord is His Name (Exodus 15:3; Jeremiah 33:2; Amos 5:8).
   c. I am the Lord (Isaiah 42:8).

2. What is the Son's name?

- a. "And she shall bring forth a son, and thou shalt call his name Jesus (Matthew 1:21)".
- b. Jesus is the "Son of God" (I John 4:15; 1st John 5:5).

3. What is the Holy Spirit's name?
   - a. The Holy Spirit's name is taken from the Hebrew name "Ruach," which means wind or spirit of God. The Greek word "Christos" translated the name as Christ, the "Anointed One."
   - b. Jesus was anointed with the Holy Spirit (Acts 10:38).
   - c. The Spirit descended upon Jesus at His baptism. Until this time, He was known as Jesus the Nazarene. He became Jesus Christ, the "Anointed One" (Matthew 3:16,17).
   - d. The Holy Spirit is spoken of as the "anointing" (I John 2:20, NIV)

STUDY QUESTIONS

1. What is water baptism?
   _____
   _____
   _____
   _____

2. What preparation is necessary for baptism?
   _____
   _____
   _____
   _____

3. What is accomplished in water baptism?

_____
_____
_____

4. What is "circumcision of the heart?"

_____
_____
_____

5. What is the "old nature?"

_____
_____
_____

6. What is meant by the term "newness of life?"

_____
_____
_____

7. What does it mean to be baptized in the name of the Lord Jesus Christ?

_____
_____
_____

FOUNDATIONS OF FAITH
HOLY SPIRIT BAPTISM

The Baptism in the Holy Spirit is a biblical theme that has suffered much abuse from many teachers. It is hoped that this lesson will assist the believer in coming to a clear understanding of the witness of the Scriptures concerning the ministry of the Holy Spirit in the Church today. The Baptism in the Holy Spirit is a complete immersion of the believer in the Holy Spirit. This Baptism grants us an entrance into the realm of spiritual power and endowment from on high (Acts 1:8; Luke 24:49).

1. WHO IS THE HOLY SPIRIT?

The Holy Spirit is not a mere influence or power. He is the third personality of the Godhead (I John 5:7; Acts 5:3,4).

1. He is a person, for He:
    a. Speaks (Acts 13:2).
    b. Works (I Corinthians 12:11).
    c. Teaches (John 14:26).
    d. Guides (John 16:13).

2. He has these human characteristics:
    a. Mind (Romans 8:27).
    b. Will (I Corinthians 12:11).
    c. Intelligence (Nehemiah 9:20).
    d. Love (Romans 15:30).
    e. Grief (Ephesians 4:30).

2. HOW IS THE HOLY SPIRIT SYMBOLICALLY REPRESENTED IN THE SCRIPTURES?

1. Dove (Matthew 3:16).

2. Water (John 4:14; John 7:38,39; Isaiah 44:3, 55:1).

3. Rain (Joel 2:23).

4. Oil (Psalm 89:20).

5. Wind (John 3:8; Acts 2:2).

6. Fire (Luke 3:16; Isaiah 4:4; Acts 2:3).

3. WHAT OTHER NAMES ARE USED FOR THE HOLY SPIRIT?

1. Spirit of the Lord, Spirit of Wisdom, Spirit of Understanding, Spirit of Council, Spirit of Might, Spirit of Knowledge, and Spirit of the Fear of the Lord (Isaiah 11:2).

2. Spirit of Christ (I Peter 1:11).

3. Spirit of Prophecy (Revelations 19:10).

4. Spirit of Glory (I Peter 4:14).

5. Comforter (John 14:26).

6. Eternal Spirit (Hebrews 9:14).

7. Spirit of Promise (Ephesians 1:13).

4. WHAT IS THE HISTORICAL SETTING FOR THE BAPTISM IN THE HOLY SPIRIT?

1. The Holy Spirit used people under the Old Covenant:
    a. Bezaleel (Exodus 35:30,31).
    b. Samson (Judges 15:14).

c. David (Matthew 22:43).
   d. The Old Testament Prophets (II Peter 1:21).

2. It was a prophetic promise of the Old Covenant:
   a. Spirit to be poured out upon thy seed (Isaiah 44:3).
   b. New Spirit put within (Ezekiel 36:26).

3. Spirit to be poured out on all flesh (Joel 2:28,29).

4. Spirit of grace and supplication to be poured out (Zechariah 12:10).

5. The New Testament testifies to the authenticity of the Holy Spirit Baptism:
   a. John the Baptist referred to the Baptism of the Holy Ghost (Mark 1:8).
   b. Jesus commended the apostles to wait in Jerusalem to receive it (Luke 24:49; Acts 1:4,5).
   c. Peter refers to the promise of the Holy Ghost on the Day of Pentecost (Acts 2:33).

6. It was not a promise intended only for the early Church (Acts 2:39):
   a. It was a promise unto you (those present).
   b. To your children (future generation).
   c. To all who are afar off (Acts 2:39).

God makes the baptism in the Holy Spirit available to all. He has not limited this provision to a "select" few.

5. HOW DOES ONE KNOW WHEN HE HAS RECEIVED THE HOLY SPIRIT BAPTISM?

1. On the Day of Pentecost, believers spoke in tongues (Acts 2:4).

2. The Samaritans received a power that was visible (Acts 8:14-25).

3. The Holy Spirit fell on all at Cornelius' house (Acts 10:44-46).

4. Jesus said we would speak with new tongues if we believed (Mark 16:17).

5. The Ephesians elders spoke with other tongues and prophesied (Acts 19:16).

The references relate speaking in tongues to the Holy Spirit Baptism. The evidence of the Holy Spirit Baptism is speaking with tongues.

6. WHY TONGUES?

1. Means of communication and a sign of God's presence in our lives (I Corinthians 14:2; Psalm 51:11).

2. Sign and means of restoration to the Church:
   a. God confounded the language of men because of a lack of relationship with Him (Genesis 11:1-9).
   b. God used tongues as a means of restoration and a uniting factor to the church on the Day of Pentecost (Acts 2:1-4).

7. HOW DOES THE BELIEVER RECEIVE THE BAPTISM OF THE HOLY SPIRIT?

These are two distinct methods by which the Holy Ghost was imparted:

1. Sovereign act of God (Acts 2:2-4; Acts 10:44-46).

2. Laying on of hands (Acts 8:14-19).

3. Though these are the two methods of receiving the Holy Ghost, the believer must:
   a. Understand and believe that the Holy Ghost Baptism is God's promise (Luke 11:13).
   b. Prepare his heart through repentance (Acts 2:38).
   c. Ask (Luke 11:13).
   d. Have faith to receive (Galatians 3:2).

8. WHAT ARE THE ADVANTAGES OF RECEIVING THE BAPTISM OF THE HOLY SPIRIT?

1. Edification (Jude 20; Romans 8:26,27; I Corinthians 14:4).

2. It gives us the power to be effective witnesses for Christ (Acts 1:8).

3. It enables us to manifest the fruits of the Spirit (Galatians 5:22,23).

4. Transforms the believer's life (Titus 3:5; II Corinthians 3:18).

5. Quickening for your mortal body (Romans 8:11).

6. Assurance of the Resurrection (Acts 2:33).

7. It enables us to taste the power of the world to come (Hebrews 6:4).

8. Provides us with a pure channel of prayer (Romans 8:26).

9. Reveals all things to us (John 14:26).

10. Perfect guidance (Romans 8:14).

The Baptism of the Holy Spirit is considered a distinct and separate experience from salvation and water baptism in New Testament Scriptures. The Word of God declares in John 1:33 that it is the ministry of Christ to baptize in the Holy Spirit. Our hearts must be ready to receive that which Christ has proposed and designed for our lives.

STUDY QUESTIONS

1. Who is the Holy Spirit?
   _____
   _____
   _____
   _____

2. What human characteristics does the Holy Spirit have?
   _____
   _____
   _____
   _____

3. What are some other names for the Holy Spirit?
   _____
   _____
   _____
   _____

4. What is the baptism of the Holy Spirit?
   _____
   _____
   _____
   _____

5.   What must we do to receive the baptism of the Holy Spirit?

_____
_____
_____
_____

6.   What does the baptism of the Holy Spirit do for the believer?

_____
_____
_____
_____

FOUNDATIONS OF FAITH
THE TRINITY OF GIVING

The principle of tithing can be traced throughout the entire Bible. In actuality, it was derived in the Garden of Eden, when mankind took something that belonged to or was designated for God (Genesis 2:16,17; 3:6). Abraham was used to initiate the tithe as we know it, giving to Melchizedek, a priest of God. Jacob also consecrated a tenth of his substance to God.

1. WHAT IS TITHING?

The tithe is the tenth of all things dedicated to sacred use. The Scripture declares that the Lord owns everything. This includes all possessions (Psalm 24:1). By tithing, we acknowledge the ownership of God over all we possess. As one pays rent to a house owner to acknowledge his ownership, we tithe to acknowledge God and His ownership. Leviticus 27:30 tells us that the tithe is holy. Holy means to be "set apart unto God." We must be conscientious to set apart that which belongs to God for His use.

2. WHAT IS THE HISTORY OF TITHING?

1. Tithing existed before the law:
    a. Abraham (Genesis 14:18-20).
    b. Jacob (Genesis 28:22).

2. Tithing existed under the law:
    a. The nation of Israel (Leviticus 27:30-33; Numbers 18:20-32).

3. Tithing existed under grace:
    a. Jesus confirmed tithing (Matthew 23:23; Luke 11:42).

    b. Tithing was not created under the law but before it (Hebrews 7:1-21).

3. IS IT NECESSARY FOR BELIEVERS TO TITHE TODAY?

1. Yes. God admonishes us to tithe (Leviticus 27:30; Proverbs 3:9,10).

2. If a person does not tithe and present offerings to God, he is robbing God (Malachi 3:8-10).

The tithe is not ours to give; it is already God's possession. If a person only tithes and does not present offerings, he is not giving anything at all to God. "Will a man rob God? Yet ye have robbed me. But ye say, Wherein have we robbed thee? In tithes and offerings. Ye are cursed with a curse: for ye have robbed me, even this whole nation. Bring ye all the tithe into the storehouse, that there may be meat in mine house and prove me now herewith, saith the Lord of hosts, if I will not open the windows of heaven and pour you out a blessing that there shall not be room enough to receive it" (Mal.3:8-10).

4. WHERE IS THE TITHE TO BE GIVEN?

1. To the storehouse of God (Malachi 3:10).

2. The storehouse is where you receive spiritual nourishment.

3. The storehouse of Israel was the Tabernacle.

4. The storehouse to the New Covenant believer is the local Church.

5. IS THE OFFERING THE SAME THING AS A TITHE?

1. No, it is a gift to God above our regular tithe.

2. It is given above and beyond that which is required.

3. The Word of God distinguishes between the two (Malachi 3:8).

6. WHAT ARE THE DIFFERENT SCRIPTURAL WAYS OF GIVING?

1. Tithes - that portion was given to God into the storehouse (the local assembly).

2. Offerings - that which is given to support other ministries.

3. Alms - that which is given as a gift to an individual.

7. WHAT ATTITUDES ARE TO BE PRESENT IN THE HEARTS OF THOSE WHO GIVE TO GOD?

1. Give "willingly" (II Corinthians 8:3, 12).

2. Give "cheerfully" (II Corinthians 9:7).

3. Give "lovingly" (II Corinthians 8:24).

4. Give "thankfully" (II Corinthians 9:11,12).

5. Give with "pure motives" (Matthew 6:2-4).

8. WHAT PRINCIPLES ARE WE TO FOLLOW IN GIVING?

1. First, we must give ourselves to the Lord (II Corinthians 8:5).

2. According to our ability (Acts 11:29; II Corinthians 8:12).

3. Give regularly (I Corinthians 16:1,2).

4. Give systematically (II Corinthians 9:7).

5. Give as a ministry to the Lord and His saints (II Corinthians 9:12,13).

6. Give as unto the Lord and not to be noticed by men (Matthew 6:2-4).

There is a principle of blessing in that God desires that we might give to release the blessing of God upon us. Our attitude always affects the situation we are involved in, so we must be ever mindful to give out of a cheerful and willing heart. God desires us to give in a manner that will bring glory to Him.

STUDY QUESTIONS

1. What is tithing?

_____
_____
_____

2. What is an offering?

_____
_____
_____

3. What are alms?

_____
_____
_____

4. Where do we tithe?

_____
_____
_____

5. Why do we tithe?

_____
_____
_____

6. What attitudes should prevail in our hearts as we give?

_____
_____
_____

FOUNDATIONS OF FAITH
PRAISE AND WORSHIP

These days, God is restoring praise and worship to the Church. Many passages of Scripture refer to these two topics. For this reason, praise and worship are the center of much conversation and study within the Church. The days are past when we took for granted that God accepted our praise and worship. Now, the Church is searching and studying the Word of God to find out what God accepts as praise and worship.

1. **WHAT ARE PRAISE AND WORSHIP?**

    1. Praise - Often, praise and thanksgiving go hand-in-hand. Thanksgiving arises from our desire to show appreciation for the goodness of God and the gifts He bestows upon us. Praise stems from the desire to love and extol God for Who He is rather than what He does.

    2. Worship - In Hebrew, it means to "bow yourself down in adoring contemplation of God." Worship involves devotion, reverence, adoration, respect, and honor.

2. **IS IT IMPORTANT THAT WE PRAISE AND WORSHIP THE LORD? YES!**

    1. The Importance of Praise:
        a. This is how we come into His presence (Psalm 100:4).
        b. God inhabits the praise of His people (Psalm 22:3).
        c. It is pleasing to God (Psalm 69:30,31).
        d. God requires it as our sacrifice to Him (Hebrew 13:15).

    2. The Importance of Worship:

a. The Word of God expresses God's desire for us to worship Him (Psalm 45:11; 86:9; 95:6).
   b. Satan realized and valued the importance of worship. When he tempted Jesus, he endeavored to get Jesus to worship him in exchange for the world's kingdoms (Matthew 4; Luke 4).

3. **WHY DO WE PRAISE THE LORD?**

   1. We were created for this purpose (Psalm 102:18).

   2. It is a command (Psalm 81:1-5).

   3. It is comely (Psalm 33:1), pleasant (Psalm 135:3), and good (Psalm 54:6; 92:1).

   4. God is worthy (Psalm 18:3; 48:1).

   5. Glorifies the Lord (Psalm 50:23).

   6. It provides us with:
      a. The abiding presence of the Lord (Psalm 68:32,33).
      b. A line of communication with God (Psalm 68:32,33).
      c. Deliverance (Psalm 42:5).
      d. Healing (Psalm 42:11).

4. **HOW ARE WE TO WORSHIP THE LORD?**

   1. In Spirit (John 4:20-26; Philippians 3:3).

   2. In Truth (John 4:24; 8:32; 17:17).

   3. In the Beauty of Holiness (I Chronicles 16:29; Psalm 29:2; 96:9).

4. In the Fear of the Lord (Psalm 5:7; Deuteronomy 10:12).

5. WHO ARE SOME BIBLICAL EXAMPLES OF WORSHIPERS?

1. Joshua (Joshua 5:14).

2. Gideon (Judges 7:15).

3. David (II Samuel 6:1-19; II Samuel 12:20).

4. Israel (II Chronicles 7:3; Nehemiah 8:6).

6. IN WHAT WAYS CAN WE PRAISE AND WORSHIP THE LORD? The Twelve Gates of Praise:

1. Singing (Psalms 100:2).

2. Shouting (Psalms 35:27; 132:9; Numbers 23:18-23).

3. Dancing (Psalm 149:3; 150:4; Jeremiah 31:12-14).

4. Leaping (II Samuel 6:16; Luke 6:23; Acts 3:8).

5. Walking or Marching (Joshua 6:3,4; Acts 3:8; Hebrews 11:30; Galatians 5:16).

6. Clapping (Psalm 47:1; Isaiah 55:12).

7. Lifting your hands (Psalm 63:4).

8. Musical Instruments (Psalm 150).

9. Running (I Kings 18:46; Galatians 5:7).

10. Laughing (Psalm 126:1,2).

11. Speaking & Singing in Tongues (I Corinthians 14:15).

12. Skipping (Psalm 29:6; Song of Solomon 2:8).

7. WHEN DO WE PRAISE AND WORSHIP THE LORD?

1. Day-by-day (II Chronicles 30:21).

2. In everything (I Thessalonians 5:18; Ephesians 5:19,20).

3. Continually (Psalm 71:6; 35:28; 34:1).

8. WHERE ARE WE TO PRAISE AND WORSHIP THE LORD?

1. In our home (Psalm 42:8; 149:5).

2. In the assembly (Psalm 22:22; 35:18; 111).

3. In the presence of non-believers (Psalm 40:3; 126:2; Acts 2:46,47).

God desires the praise of His people. When we learn to praise God, we take our eyes off ourselves, and our praise ushers us into His presence. Only in His presence can we worship Him. The people of God are a spiritual house whose purpose is to show forth the praise of God (I Peter 2:9).

STUDY QUESTIONS

1. What is praise?
_____
_____
_____
_____

2. What is worship?
_____
_____
_____
_____

3. Why are praise and worship important?
_____
_____
_____
_____

4. How are we to worship the Lord?
_____
_____
_____
_____

5. In what ways can we express our praise and worship?
_____
_____
_____

6. When and where are we to praise and worship?
_____
_____
_____

FOUNDATIONS OF FAITH
FRUIT & GIFTS OF THE SPIRIT

There is a vital relationship between the fruit and the gifts of the Spirit. The fruit of the Spirit is the practical manifestation of Christ in the believer's life: it offers evidence of the reality of Jesus within. The gifts of the Spirit have to do with spiritual abilities and are endowments bestowed upon the believer by God. As the word "fruit" suggests, the fruit of the Spirit takes time to develop while God freely gives the gifts. Paul's writings in the New Testament indicate that though we may have a gift given to us by God, it is of little use without His character developed within us.

1.   WHAT IS THE FRUIT OF THE SPIRIT?

Galatians 5:22 tells us that the fruit of the Spirit is the character of God in us...

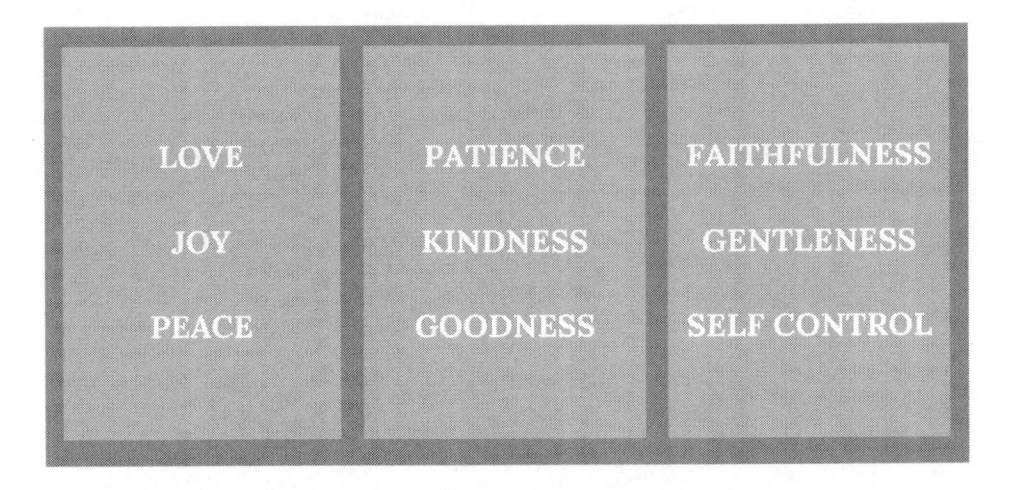

LOVE	PATIENCE	FAITHFULNESS
JOY	KINDNESS	GENTLENESS
PEACE	GOODNESS	SELF CONTROL

"Fruit" is used metaphorically to mean "result or outcome." In other words, the result or outcome of the Holy Spirit in the believer's life should be the nine virtues listed above. Vine defines fruit as "the visible expression of power working inwardly and invisibly, the fruit's character being evidence of the power producing it."

2. HOW ARE THESE VIRTUES BROUGHT ABOUT IN OUR LIVES?

1. By the Gospel (Colossians 1:5,6).

2. By being joined to Christ (Romans 7:4).

3. By abiding in Christ and allowing ourselves to be pruned (John 15:2-16).

4. Tribulation (Romans 5:3).

5. Meditating on God's Word (Psalm 1:2).

6. Rejecting the counsel and company of the ungodly (Psalm 1:1).

7. By walking as "children of the light" (Ephesians 5:7-9).

8. Not providing the flesh and dying to self (Romans 13:14; John 12:24).

9. We should allow ourselves to be trained by chastening (Hebrews 12:11).

3. HOW IMPORTANT IS "FRUIT BEARING" FOR A BELIEVER?

1. It is for this purpose that Jesus chose us (John 15:16).

2. Scripture tells us that repentance will cause fruit to come forth in our lives (Matthew 3:8).

3. We are warned of the danger of not bearing fruit (Matthew 3:10; 25:14-30; Hebrews 6:7,8).

4. Paul, in I Corinthians 13:1-3, proclaims the emptiness of exercising spiritual gifts without the love of God motivating him.

4.   WHAT ARE THE GIFTS OF THE SPIRIT?

I Corinthians 12:4-11 lists nine Gifts of the Spirit, which can be grouped into three major divisions:

1. Revelation Gifts:
    a. Word of Wisdom: Divine revelation of the mind and will of God, or how to carry that will out (Acts 18:9-11).
    b. Word of Knowledge: Divine knowledge concerning a person(s), place(s), or thing(s) (Acts 13:11).
    c. Discerning of Spirits: A specialized gift of knowledge to identify evil spirits or discern hypocrisy (Acts 16:16-18

2. Utterance Gifts - Tongues
    a. Prophecy comes from the Greek word "propheteia," meaning the speaking forth of the mind and counsel of God. It is not necessarily, nor even primarily, foretelling; it can be about the past, present, or future (Acts 13:2; 21:11). A prophet is simply a spokesman for God.
    b. The divine gifts of speaking in another language without its being learned (Acts 2:3-11; I Corinthians 14:22).

* **NOTE:** This is not to be confused with the devotional gift of tongues, a means of private communication between a believer's spirit and God (I Corinthians 14:2; Jude 20; Ephesians 6:18).

3. Interpretation of Tongues: The divine enablement to explain the meaning of a message given in tongues (I Corinthians 14:10-13).

4. Power Gifts
   a. Faith: (Speaking about the "gift," and not general faith) it is the ability given by the Holy Spirit to believe God to do the impossible (Acts 3:1-7; 27:25).
   b. Healings: The ability given by the Holy Spirit to impart healing to a person's physical body. This is not human or soulish power, but the Holy Spirit flowing through a willing vessel (Acts 28:8). It is not necessary that hands be used for this gift to be operational (Acts 19:11,12).
   c. Working of Miracles: (Literal Greek - "operations of power"). The ability given by the Holy Spirit to perform works of a divine origin and character, such as could not be produced by natural agents and means (Acts 3:12, 6:8, 14:3).

5. CAN THE BELIEVER MOVE IN ONLY ONE OF THE GIFTS?

1. The scripture indicates that an individual may function in one gift in particular or in more than one.

2. It can also be seen from the examples and definitions of the gifts that several gifts are often in operation simultaneously. (Faith with healing and miracles, word of knowledge with prophecy).

6. WHY ARE THE GIFTS GIVEN TO THE CHURCH?

1. For the common good (I Corinthians 12:7).

2. Edification (I Corinthians 14:3,5).

3. To convict and convince (I Corinthians 14:24,25).

4. Instruction and exhortation (I Corinthians 14:31).

The fruit and gifts of the Holy Spirit are important endowments for the individual believer and the Body of Christ. The fruit of the spirit testifies to the divine exchange as Christ's character and nature prevail in the believer's life. The gifts help build up and establish the Body of Christ and meet the church's spiritual and physical needs (I Corinthians 14:12 and 12:7).

STUDY QUESTIONS

1. What is the fruit of the spirit?

_____
_____
_____

2. How do we develop the fruit of the Spirit in our lives?

_____
_____
_____

3. Why is it important for the believer to bear fruit?

_____
_____
_____

4. What are the gifts of the Spirit?
_____
_____
_____
_____

5. Why are the gifts of the Spirit given to the Church?

_____
_____
_____
_____

FOUNDATIONS OF FAITH
PROPHECY IN THE CHURCH TODAY

The prophetic ministry has been established to communicate God's purposes to man through the ages. God is still speaking to man and making His will known through written and spoken or prophetic words. Together, they testify and bear witness to one another, motivating and equipping the believer to fulfill God's call upon his life.

1. **WHAT IS PROPHECY?**

    1. Prophecy is the communication of God's thoughts and intentions to mankind.

    2. The Bible, as a whole, can be considered prophecy (II Peter 1:21; II Timothy 3:16).

    3. Prophecy is one of the nine manifestations of the Holy Spirit (I Corinthians 14:1,5,24,25,39).

    4. The ministry or office of the prophet is one of the "fivefold" ministries given to the church to help equip and develop the saints (Ephesians 4:11-16).

2. **ARE THERE DIFFERENT EXPRESSIONS OF PROPHECY? - YES!**

    1. The office of the prophet (Ephesians 2:20; 4:11; Acts 13:1).

    2. *This is a particular investment of Christ's mantle or impartation of God's wisdom, nature, and power.* This is a higher realm of ministry than one that operates in the "gifts of prophecy" within the body of believers.

    3. Prophetic Presbytery (I Timothy 4:14).

a. Used to reveal and confirm those called to leadership in the church.
   b. Used to impart spiritual gifts and callings.
   c. Used to confirm and activate ministries in the Body of Christ.

4. Gifts of Prophecy (Acts 2:17; I Corinthians 12:10; 14:1,3-5,22,24,31,39).

5. The gift of prophecy is a divine enablement for the edification of the Body of Christ (I Peter 4:10).

6. The spirit of prophecy (Numbers 11:24-30; I Samuel 10:10).

7. The anointing of Christ arises within the believer and is evident when Christians exercise their faith to be a voice through which Christ can testify.

8. The song of the Lord (Colossians 3:16).

9. Song is used prophetically to express the thoughts and desires of Christ. Prophetic preaching (I Peter 4:11). The minister is used as an "oracle of God" through the prophetic anointing. The words, scriptures, and illustrations used in the sermon represent the voice of God.

3. WHAT IS PERSONAL PROPHECY?

Personal prophecy is used to communicate the mind of Christ to individual members of the body of Christ. It provides direction, motivation, instruction, impartation, and even correction for the individual.

1. It will not conflict with truths or principles of God already established in the scriptures (Deuteronomy 13:1-3).

2. Personal Prophecy is:
    a. Partial (I Corinthians 13:8,9). It reveals only a portion of God's will for our lives. It does not outline every detail God has in store for us.
    b. Progressive (See the life of Abraham outlined in Genesis) God may reveal His plan for our lives as we walk per that which we already know to be God's will. Piece by piece, bit by bit, His plan unfolds.
    c. Conditional (I Samuel 13:13-15). The fulfillment of the prophetic word is dependent on human response to the Word of the Lord.

4.   WHAT SHOULD OUR RESPONSE BE TO PERSONAL PROPHECY?

1. Record the prophecy, read, and meditate on the Word of the Lord (I Timothy 4:14,15).

2. Receive it with faith (Hebrews 11:6; Mark 9:23).

3. Be a "doer of the Word" (James 1:22; Deuteronomy 29:29).

4. Seek for God's timing in fulfillment of the Word.

5. Be submitted to "seasoned ministry" and seek guidance and counsel on how and when the Word of the Lord will be implemented in your life.

The prophetic ministry is but one of the ways that God chooses to communicate and confirm His will to man. The prophetic word must always be tested and judged by the individual, seasoned ministry, and the written Word.

STUDY QUESTIONS

1. What is prophecy?
   _____
   _____
   _____
   _____

2. What are the different expressions of prophecy?
   _____
   _____
   _____
   _____

3. What is personal prophecy?
   _____
   _____
   _____
   _____

4. What is the nature of personal prophecy?
   _____
   _____
   _____
   _____

5. How are we to respond to personal prophecy?
   _____
   _____
   _____
   _____

FOUNDATIONS OF FAITH
PRAYER AND FASTING

We find men and women who have a personal and intimate relationship with God throughout the Word of God. Prayer and fasting are two keys to developing and maintaining intimacy with God. Communication with the Lord is dependent upon our prayer life. Fasting helps to discipline our bodies and souls to hear from God. It does not "buy" us anything from God but aligns our hearts before the Lord, knowing that we serve a God who understands our every need (Psalm 62:8).

1. WHAT IS THE MEANING PRAYER?

Several words are translated as "pray" or "prayer" in the Old and New Testaments. Some of the English words that are associated with prayer are "entreaty," "intercession," and "supplication."

1. Prayer is a time of communion and fellowship with the Lord. This includes:
   a. Our speaking to the Lord.
   b. The Lord is addressing us as well. "... They called upon the Lord, and He answered them. He spake unto them..." (Psalm 99:6).

2. Prayer is a continual relationship (Ephesians 6:18; I Thessalonians 5:17).

2. WHAT ARE SOME BIBLICAL EXAMPLES OF PRAYER?

Both the Old and New Testaments provide us with examples:

1. Hannah (I Samuel 1:27).

2. Solomon (I Kings 8:22-26).

3. Jesus (Luke 5:15,16; 22:42,43).

4. Paul (Ephesians 3:14).

5. A single individual or a group may participate in prayer:
    a. An individual (Matthew 6:5-7).
    b. Two or three (Matthew 18:18-20).
    c. A corporate body or church (Acts 2:42; 4:24).

3. WHAT ARE THE KEYS TO EFFECTIVE PRAYER?

In Matthew 6:9-13 and Luke 11:1-3, we find the disciples inquiring of Jesus concerning their prayer life. The prayer Jesus gives them gives us a pattern for our prayer life today.

1. "Our Father which art in heaven hallowed be Thy Name" gives us insight into our relationship and the promises that are ours as we know His name.

2. "Thy Kingdom come, Thy will be done" helps us establish God's kingdom as our priority and understand what will occur in and on this earth.

3. "Give us this day our daily bread": The Father makes provision for our every need.

4. "Forgive us our trespasses as we forgive our trespassers": We must maintain right relationships with one another to keep our relationship with the Lord vital and fresh.

5. "Lead us not into temptation, but deliver us from evil": God's power is greater than the enemy's. This will help us to defeat Satan effectively.

6. "For Thine is the Kingdom, the Power, and the Glory": How to have a dynamic encounter with the living God.

4. WHAT OTHER PRINCIPLES ARE WE TO FOLLOW IN PRAYER?

1. Be following God's will (I John 5:14,15).

2. It should be made with thanksgiving (Psalm 100:4).

3. It should not be a mere ritual or vain repetition (Matthew 6:7).

4. We must pray in faith, nothing wavering (James 1:6-8).

5. ARE THERE DIFFERENT KINDS OF PRAYER?

Yes, 1st Timothy 2:1 gives us insight into this; it mentions supplications, prayer intercessions, and giving thanks.

1. Supplication: Means to beseech, beg, plead, or appeal to God (Daniel 9; Ephesians 6:18).

2. Prayers: Any type of communication between God and man. This includes waiting before God in silence, making petitions of Him, seeking His face, and even calling upon His name (Isaiah 40:31; I Chronicles 4:10; II Chronicles 26:5).

3. Intercession: When we plead in favor of a person or cause before God (Exodus 32:10-14; Genesis 18:22,23; Luke 23:34).

4. Giving of Thanks: Coming before God with "an attitude of gratitude" (Psalm 100:4; Philippians 4:6).

5. Praying in the Holy Ghost: Praying in the unction and power of the Holy Spirit (Jude 20; Ephesians 6:18; I Corinthians 14:14,15).

6. WHAT ARE SOME HINDRANCES TO PRAYER?

1. Undisciplined thoughts (II Corinthians 10:4-5).

2. Asking amiss (James 4:1-3).

3. Unforgiveness (Matthew 5;7,23,24, 18:21-35).

4. Pride (Psalm 138:6).

5. Unforgiven sin and iniquity (Psalm 66:18; Isaiah 59:1-4).

6. Bitterness (Hebrews 12:12-17).

7. Unbelief (James 1:5-7).

8. Improper relationship (I Peter 3:7).

7. WHAT IS FASTING?

Fasting is deliberately turning from food and/or personal appetites so that we might focus on God.

8. WHAT ARE THE RESULTS OF PRAYER AND FASTING?

1. Daniel received divine instruction (Daniel 10).

2. The city of Nineveh was saved (Jonah 3).

3. The nation of Israel was delivered from death (Esther 4).

4. Demons cast out (Matthew 17:14-21).

5. The will of God is revealed (Acts 9:9-15; 13:1-4).

6. The elders of the church were chosen and ordained (Acts 14:23).

9. THERE ARE BLESSINGS PROMISED TO THOSE WHO FAST AND PRAY:

1. Isaiah 58:6-12 gives the benefits of prayer and fasting with the right motives.

2. Disciplines our body, subdues the flesh, and allows our spirit to be strengthened (I Corinthians 9:27).

3. Ministers unto the Lord (Acts 13:1-3).

4. It gives power to do spiritual warfare (Matthew 17:21).

10. ARE THERE DIFFERENT TYPES OF FASTS? - YES!

1. Regular fast: refraining from all food and drink except water (Matthew 4:1-3).

2. Partial Fast: Refraining from a certain meal or restricting the intake of certain foods (Daniel 10:3).

3. Complete Fast: Refraining from all food and liquid (Acts 9:9; Esther 4:16).

11. WHEN ARE WE TO FAST?

1. When led or directed by the Spirit of the Lord (Matthew 4;1,2).

2. When, as individuals, we sense the need (Matthew 6:16-18).

3. When the Church, as a body, is called to fast (Joel 1:14; 2:15,16).

Prayer and fasting are two essential tools for waging spiritual warfare. As we approach God with the right motives in our hearts and our minds focused on Him, we can expect results from the petitions we lift before Him (I John 5:14,15).

STUDY QUESTIONS

1. What is prayer?

_____
_____
_____
_____

2. Give two keys essential for effective prayer.

_____
_____
_____
_____

3. What is fasting?

_____
_____
_____
_____

4. What results can we expect when we fast and pray?
___
___
___
___

5. How do we prepare our hearts and minds for prayer and fasting?
___
___
___
___

FOUNDATIONS OF FAITH
COMMUNION AND DIVINE HEALING

Communion is a vital aspect of life within the church of the Lord Jesus Christ. It is an act through which we "remember the work of the Lord Jesus Christ" (I Corinthians 11:23-26). The communion meal involves many important provisions; divine healing is but one. Through this lesson, we will explore both the meanings and benefits of partaking in the covenant meal.

1. WHAT IS THE MEANING OF THE WORD "COMMUNION?"

The word means "act of sharing, communication, unity, concord, agreement, joint participation."

2. WHAT IS THE ORIGIN OF THE COMMUNION MEAL?

1. Jesus initiated the celebration of the communion meal with His disciples before His crucifixion (Matthew 26:26-28; Mark 14:22-24).

2. Jesus proclaimed this to be a meal through which He would be brought to the remembrance of His followers (Luke 22:17-20).

3. Jesus and His disciples ate this meal before He became the fulfillment of the Passover Lamb (Exodus 12:1-14).
    a. Jesus is called the "Lamb of God" (John 1:29).
    b. Christ called "our Passover" (I Corinthians 5:7).
    c. Christ called the "Lamb without spot or blemish" (I Peter 1:19).

4. Paul received a distinct revelation concerning the covenant meal (I Corinthians 11:23-32).

3. WHAT DO THE ELEMENTS OF COMMUNION REPRESENT?

1. The Bread:
    a. Jesus body, which He allowed to be broken for us (Luke 22:19; I John 3:16; Isaiah 53:4-6).
    b. The body of Christ is the Church Universal of which each believer is a part (I Corinthians 10:16,17; 12:12,13).
    c. By partaking in the bread, we acknowledge participation in the sacrifice of the cross (Galatians 2:20; 6:14; Romans 6:6-11).
    d. Unleavened bread is the Body of Christ (Matthew 26:17-19).

2. The Wine:
    a. Christ's Blood:
        i. Of the New Covenant (Matthew 26:28; Hebrews 9:11-14).
        ii. Shed on behalf of many (Matthew 20:28; 26:28).
        iii. For forgiveness of sins (Matthew 26:28; Romans 5:9; I John 1:7; Ephesians 1:7).
    b. It can also be representative of the Holy Spirit, who gives us life.
    c. The blood has a voice (Genesis 4:10).
        i. For the children of Israel, as they smeared it on their doorposts, it brought them out of Egyptian bondage (Exodus 12:21-23).
        ii. For the believer today, it speaks of better things (Hebrews 12:24). It provides freedom from sin, sickness, and disease.

4. HOW ARE WE TO RECEIVE COMMUNION?

1. As a believer: Because it shows a sharing in the body and blood of the Lord, the communicant must have experientially received the atoning work of Christ in his life (MUST BE "BORN AGAIN").

2. One must not partake in an unworthy manner and must:
   a. Examine (or prove himself). Upon examination, if something is not right, fix it before proceeding with the Lord's Supper (I Corinthians 11:28).
   b. Properly discern what the supper represents and believe a life consistent with what it represents (I Corinthians 11:29).

5. WHAT ARE THE BENEFITS OF COMMUNION?

1. When we drink the cup, we share in the blood of Christ (I Corinthians 10:16).

2. We are all made to drink a cup of blessing (I Corinthians 12:13).

3. As we partake of communion, we drink a cup of blessing (I Corinthians 10:16).

4. Healing is a provision for the believer in communion. (Psalm 105:37).
   a. God promises healing to the believer (Isaiah 53:3-5; Matthew 8:16,17; I Peter 2:24).
   b. Biblical examples of healing: Brazen serpent (Number 21); Healing covenant given (Exodus 15:26); Jesus healed all that were sick (Matthew 8:16); Apostles given the power and authority to heal (Mark 16:17-20; Acts 3:1-8).

c. There are different ways to be healed: Personal prayer (James 5:16); Prayer by the elders (James 5:14,15); Laying-On of Hands (Mark 16:17,18); Sending the Word (Psalm 107:20); The table of the Lord (I Corinthians 11:23-32); Prayer cloths (Acts 19:12); Gifts of the Spirit (I Corinthians 12:9,10); Praise and Worship (Psalm 32:7; 8:1,2: Matthew 21:12-16).

6. CONSEQUENCES OF DRINKING UNWORTHILY:

1. Guilty of the body and the blood of the Lord.

2. He eats and drinks judgment upon himself.

3. Will reap weakness and sickness.

We see communion as partaking of the body and blood of Jesus Christ. It is not a mere ritual.

STUDY QUESTIONS

1. What is the origin of the communion meal?

_____
_____
_____
_____

2. What does the bread represent?

_____
_____
_____
_____

3. What does the wine represent?

_____
_____
_____

4. How do we prepare to receive communion?

_____
_____
_____

5. What are the benefits of communion?

_____
_____
_____

6. What are the ways to receive healing?

_____
_____
_____

THE CHURCH
THE CHURCH

The church is the divinely ordained body responsible for nurturing believers and preaching the gospel. It is the expression of the Kingdom of God on the earth. The word "church," from the Greek text, means: "assembly, gathering meeting." It is used by the Christian church or congregation. It means a "calling out of." This message is conveyed to us in II Corinthians 6:17.

1. WHAT IS THE CHURCH?

1. The Church is a group of born-again believers meeting together to worship God, be trained in God's kingdom, and minister the gospel to the world.

2. The church is not a literal building but a body of redeemed people (I Corinthians 12:27).

3. The church is not a denomination or sect:
   a. There is no scripture authorizing the present divisions in Christianity.
   b. The New Testament Church is not to be divided by anything.
   c. The Church must reach every society, every nation, every language, and every person.

2. WHAT ARE THE MAIN ASPECTS OF THE CHURCH?

1. The Church is "invisible" (Hebrews 12:22,23). This speaks of unity within a spiritual body for the habituation of God by the Spirit, with Jesus as the Head. It is not spoken of in a visible sense but is an invisible union of all true believers in Jesus Christ (Ephesians 2:19-22; I Corinthians 3:16).

2. The Church is "visible."
   a. Groups of believers in a given location (Matthew 18:20).
   b. Believers gathered to the person of Jesus for worship (John 4:24).
   c. Live a disciplined life of prayer and unity (Matthew 18:19,20; I Thessalonians 5:17).
   d. Being edified or built up by the five-fold ministry (Ephesians 4:11-16).
   e. Established in the principles of Christ's doctrine (Acts 2:42).
   f. Centrally governed, yet in fellowship with other believers (Revelations 1:11; Philippians 1:1).

3. **WHAT ARE SOME OF THE OTHER NAMES IN SCRIPTURE BY WHICH THE NEW TESTAMENT CHURCH IS CALLED?**

   1. Temple: Jesus is the Chief Cornerstone (Eph. 2:19-22; I Peter 2:5-7).

   2. Family: Jesus, the Head (Ephesians 3:14,15).

   3. Bride: Jesus, the Bridegroom (Ephesians 5:22-32).

   4. Army: Jesus, the Captain (Ephesians 6:10-17).

   5. Body: Jesus, the Head (Ephesians 1:22,23; 4:16).

   6. City: Jesus, the Light (Matthew 5:14; Hebrews 11:10; 12:22.23).

   7. Vineyard: Jesus, the Vine (John 15:1-7).

   8. Sheepfold: Jesus, the Shepherd (John 10:1-16).

9. Holy Nation: Jesus, the Firstborn (I Peter 2:9; Romans 8:29).

10. Holy Priesthood: Jesus, the High Priest (I Peter 2:5,9; Hebrews 7).

4. **WHAT IS THE LOCAL CHURCH?**

   1. It is the local assembly of members of the Body of Christ. Their common bond is their fellowship with the Lord Jesus Christ (I Corinthians 1:1-2; I Thessalonians 1:1; Galatians 1:1-2).

   2. Its mission is to proclaim and demonstrate the Lord Jesus Christ's message and ministry (Matthew 28:18-20; Mark 16:15-18; John 17:13-18).

   3. The local church allows the believers to edify or build up one another (Romans 14:19; I Thessalonians 5:11).

   4. It is a command in the scriptures for believers to attach themselves to a body of believers (Hebrews 10:23-25).

5. **WHAT IS THE "GOVERNING" STRUCTURE WITHIN THE LOCAL CHURCH?**

   1. Church government is necessary to provide order, maintain peace among brethren, and instill obedience to God's will (I Corinthians 12:28; Hebrews 13:17).

   2. Christ is the head of the Church, both universal and local (Ephesians 5:23; Colossians 1:12-18, 2:19).

   3. Under Christ, various ministries serve to perfect the body of Christ (I Corinthians 12:28; Ephesians 4:11,12).

4. Elders are the ruling authorities in the local church (I Timothy 3:1-7).

6. WHAT IS THE OFFICE OF THE ELDER?

1. The qualifications to meet the office of the Elder are outlined in I Timothy 3:1-7 and Titus 1:5-7.

2. An Elder must meet high moral, civil, and spiritual standards.

3. There are various terms synonymous with the word "Elder" in the New Testament:
    a. Elder: taken from the Greek "presbuteros," which means "senior." This refers to the personal status of the bishop (I Peter 5:1-5).
        i. The elder's function is to rule (I Timothy 5:17-21).
        ii. They have responsibility and accountability for the flock (Hebrews 13:17).
    b. Pastor: taken from the Greek "poimen," which means "shepherd." This one feeds, protects, and instructs (Ephesians 4:11,12; Jeremiah 23:4).
    c. Elders are to lead by example at all times and in all scenarios.
    d. Be faithful in attendance and tithing and support the pastor's and staff's vision.

7. WHAT IS THE OFFICE OF A DEACON?

1. The qualifications to meet the office of deacon are outlined in Acts 6:3 and I Timothy 3:8-13.

2. The deacon must meet the highest moral, civil, and spiritual standards.

3. The word "deacon" is taken from the Greek "diakonos," meaning "servant" or "helper."

4. A deacon serves as an official to carry out various "duties" within the local church.

Through the Church, believers are nurtured and brought to maturity in Christ. The local church provides fellowship and is the training ground to equip believers to proclaim the gospel to the "uttermost parts of the earth."

STUDY QUESTIONS

1. What is the church?

_____
_____
_____
_____

2. What is the mission of the church?

_____
_____
_____
_____

3. What is the relationship between the Lord Jesus and His church?

_____
_____
_____
_____

4. Why is the local church important?
_____
_____
_____
_____

THE CHURCH
FELLOWSHIP

The word "fellowship" is found many times throughout the Bible. We are called unto the fellowship of Jesus Christ (I Corinthians 1:9). We are also admonished to refrain from fellowshipping with non-believers and workers of unrighteousness. In this lesson, we hope to establish what bonds are created between the fellowship of born-again believers and also point out those they are not to include in their fellowship.

1. WHAT DOES THE WORD "FELLOWSHIP" MEAN?

There are three Greek words used for fellowship in the New Testament:

1. KOINONIA: meaning "close association; communion; close relationship." It is the most frequently used word for fellowship. This speaks of the act of using a thing in common.

2. METOCHE: "partnership; a holding with; a sharing."

3. SUGKOINONED: "a joint partaker with."

2. WITH WHOM ARE WE TO FELLOWSHIP?

There are two aspects of fellowship found in the Word of God. For the benefit of the fellowship to be complete, we must be active participants in both aspects.

1. First, YOU MUST BE IN FELLOWSHIP WITH GOD:

2. This is expressed through prayer, praise, worship, and obedience to God.

  a. "Our fellowship is with the Father" (I John 1:3).
  b. "Called unto the fellowship of His Son Jesus Christ our Lord.: (I Corinthians 1:9).
  c. "Fellowship of the Spirit" (Philippians 2:1).

3. Then YOU MUST BE IN FELLOWSHIP WITH THE BODY OF BELIEVERS:

4. It is vital, both for the body of Christ and the individual believer, for fellowship to be a part of Church life.
  a. "But if we walk in the light, as He is in the light, we have fellowship one with another..." (I John 1:7)
  b. The fellowship of believers is to prosper both the individual and the Body of Christ in two ways: spiritually and practically. Acts 2:42-47 gives us a pattern for fellowship. We are to:
    i. Be diligent and consistent in hearing and doing the Word of God (Acts 2:42).
    ii. Have fellowship in communion (Acts 2:42-47).
    iii. Have all things in common (speaking of material wealth) (Acts 2:44,45; Romans 12:13).
    iv. Be in one accord with singleness of heart (having no discord or strife) (Acts 2:46).
    v. Abound in praise and thanksgiving (Acts 2:47).

Fellowship not only meets life's spiritual needs but also social needs (Acts 2:46; Romans 12:13; Hebrews 13:16 NIV). God intended that the Church have a balanced lifestyle that would minister to every area of human need.

 5. Fellowship with God and the brethren go hand in hand.

4. With whom are we not allowed to fellowship?
_____
_____
_____
_____

THE CHURCH
THE SHEEP AND THE SHEPHERD

There has been much teaching on the role of the pastor and his relationship to those God has placed in his congregation. There has been much hurt caused by imbalanced teaching. Throughout the Bible, God's people are referred to as "sheep" (Psalms 79:13; 100:3), and sheep need a shepherd to both feed and tend to their measures that advocate "Lording" over every aspect of the lives of the congregation instead of leading the sheep. However, we must also be careful not to miss the fullness of God's purpose for His church by failing to submit to a local church body and pastor.

1. **WHAT IS A SHEPHERD?**

The word "shepherd" is used in both the Old and New Testaments. It means "one who tends herds or flocks" (not merely one who feeds them). Hebrews and Greek words, translated as "shepherd," are also translated as "pastor."

2. **IS JESUS THE ONLY SHEPHERD?**

    1. Jesus is spoken of as the "Chief Shepherd" (John 10:11,14; Hebrews 13:20; I Peter 5:4; 2:25).

    2. Jeremiah prophesied that the Lord would set up shepherds over His people (Jeremiah 23:3-4).

    3. Pastors or shepherds were given to the Church as a gift (Ephesians 4:11).

3. **WHAT ARE THE DUTIES OF A SHEPHERD?**

    1. We can tell by the indictment against the Old Testament shepherd what the Lord expects (Ezekiel 34:2-4):

a. Feed the flock.
   b. Strengthen the diseased.
   c. Heal the sick.
   d. Bind up the broken.
   e. Bring back those who were driven away.
   f. Seek for the lost.
   g. Not rule with force or cruelty.

2. Jeremiah prophesied that His shepherd would (Jeremiah 3:15):
   a. Be shepherds after His own heart.
   b. Feed the sheep knowledge and understanding.

3. The New Testament scriptures tell us:
   a. He calls his sheep by name, leads them, and goes before them (John 10:3,4).
   b. He will lay down his life for his sheep (John 10:11-13).
   c. He is on guard for himself and his sheep against the wolves and will give account for them (Acts 20:28,29; Hebrews 13:17)
   d. He will willingly oversee his flock and not be motivated by greed (I Peter 5:2).
   e. He will provide an example for his flock (I Peter 5:3).
   f. He will help to equip the saints for the work of the ministry (Ephesians 4:7-13)

4. **WHAT VALUE DOES GOD PLACE ON HIS SHEEP?**

1. Luke 15:4-7 depicts the parable of "The Lost Sheep." We see that God considered one lost sheep worth leaving the 99. He will search it out until it is found.

2. Jesus looked upon the people of His day with compassion, for He saw them as sheep without a shepherd (Matthew 9:36).

3. The Word of God commands His people to submit to and obey those who rule over us because they watch over our souls (Hebrews 13:17; I Corinthians 16:15,16).

5. **SIX "MUSTS" FOR THE SHEEP**

    1. Must know the voice of the Shepherd.

    2. Must follow the shepherd.

    3. Must eat what the shepherd feeds.

    4. Must heed the warnings of the shepherd.

    5. Must bear fruit.

    6. Must allow the shepherd to shear them.

6. **FIVE KINDS OF SHEEP**

    1. Solitary: They stay away from the rest of the flock. They think the rest of the flock is too mature for them. They are always sick.

    2. Hermit: They stay away from the rest of the flock to avoid shearing. They refuse to be clipped by the shepherd. They won't allow the Holy Spirit to prune them. Their wool grows over their eyes, and they can't protect themselves. Their wool weighs them down, and they can't rise, so the wolves devour them. They influence others.

3. Wandering: Never content with things the way they are. Whatever God is doing is never fast enough, big enough, or good enough to suit them. They always talk about the way it "used to be." They bring discontent to other sheep and produce "like kind."

4. Judas: They lead others to the slaughter. They are usually blinded and deceived by their own stubbornness. They take an opposite stand on what the shepherd is trying to establish. They slander the shepherd. They carry tales abroad. They are unsavory, wild, and have no love for the flock.

5. Contented: Innocent - they trust the shepherd. They are mild, tender-hearted, and gracious. Patient - they stick with the flock and don't run every time things don't go their way. They are useful, industrious, and get involved. They obey and are submissive.

7. **ARE ALL THOSE IN THE FLOCK HIS SHEEP?**

1. Matthew 7:15-20 tells us there are wolves who wear sheep's clothing. They put on the appearance of sheep. We can tell or identify them by their fruit.

2. Some will separate themselves before the coming of the Lord (I John 2:19), while others will not be separated until the Lord returns (Matthew 13:30).

3. There will be those who arise from within the flock, who will speak perverse things to draw away disciples unto themselves (Acts 20:30). We are warned that there will be those who will be deceived and fall away (I Timothy 4:1).

The Scriptures indicate that the pastor or shepherd is not only responsible for preaching but also is to care for and nurture the lives of those God has placed in his congregation. The sheep, in return, must respond both to Jesus, the Chief Shepherd, and the pastor God has joined them with.

STUDY QUESTIONS

1. What is the ministry of the shepherd?

_____
_____
_____

2. What is the relationship between the shepherd and sheep?

_____
_____
_____

3. What does Luke 15 tell us about the value God places on His sheep?

_____
_____
_____

4. What are the characteristics of contented sheep?

_____
_____
_____

THE CHURCH
THE FIVE-FOLD MINISTRIES

In the previous lessons, we have seen that God has established a pattern for government within the Church. God gave Christ to the Church to be its head, and in turn, Christ has given five ministries to the Church as a gift to foster its corporate life (Ephesians 4:11-13).

1.　WHAT ARE THE FIVE MINISTRIES?

1. Apostles

2. Prophets

3. Evangelists

4. Pastors

5. Teachers

"And His gifts were that some should be apostles, some prophets, some evangelists, some pastors and teachers (Ephesians 4:11 - RSV).

2.　WHAT IS AN APOSTLE?

1. It comes from the Greek word "APOSTOLOS," meaning "one sent forth."

2. They are chosen by God, not man (Galatians 1:1; Romans 1:1,5,6).

3. Preaches the Gospel (Acts 2:14; Romans 1:1; Acts 2:14,38).

4. Testifies and exhorts (Acts 2:40).

5. Establishes doctrines (Acts 2:42).

6. Establishes churches (Acts 14:21-23).

7. Brings forth and develops those called to the ministry, giving guidance and instruction until they are confirmed into their calling (Acts 14:23).

8. Establishes believers in foundational truths.

9. Seal of apostleship of the fruit he has brought forth.

10. Has the ministry of "beginnings."

3. WHAT IS A PROPHET?

1. It comes from the Greek "PROPHETES," meaning "one who speaks forth, or openly a proclaimer of a divine message."
2. Speaks the Word of the Lord (I Corinthians 14:29).

3. Bringing forth the revelation of the Scriptures (I Corinthians 14:30).

4. Predicts and warns of the future events (Acts 11:27,28).

5. Provides direction in ministry, doctrine, and worship (Acts 13:15).

6. Confirms and imparts spiritual gifts and blessings (Acts 15:22-32).

7. Has the ministry of confirming God's motives and will.

4. **WHAT IS AN EVANGELIST?**

    1. It comes from the Greek "Eveangelistes," meaning "a messenger of good."

    2. Exhorts men to repent, believe, and obey the Gospel (II Timothy 4:2,5).

    3. Extends the message of the Gospel to unreached areas.

    4. Has the ministry of stirring.

5. **WHAT IS A PASTOR?**
    1. It comes from the Greek "Poimen," meaning a shepherd, one who tends herds or flocks (not merely one who feeds them).

    2. Feeds the flock (I Peter 5:2-4; John 21:16).

    3. Protects the flock (Acts 20:28-31).

    4. Guides the flock (John 10:3,4).

    5. Watches for the souls of those in the flock (Hebrews 13:17).

    6. He must be willing to lay down his life for his sheep (John 10:11-13).

    7. Has the ministry of feeding.

6. **WHAT IS A TEACHER?**

    1. It comes from the Greek "DIDASKALOS," meaning "master."

2. Clarifies the application of truth in our lives to enable us to be obedient to the Word of God.

3. Builds on the foundations laid by the apostles and prophets to establish the saints (I Corinthians 3).

4. Must provide motivation for studying the Scriptures.

5. Communicates revealed truth to unite the faith through understanding (I Corinthians 1:10).

6. Has the ministry of stabilizing and strengthening.

7. WHY WERE THESE MINISTRIES GIVEN TO THE CHURCH?

1. For the perfecting of the saints (Ephesians 4:12).

2. For the equipping of the saints for the work of service (Ephesians 4:12).

3. For the edifying of the body of Christ (Ephesians 4:12).

8. HOW LONG WILL THESE MINISTRIES EXIST?

Unto WE ALL come into: (Ephesians 4:13).

1. The unity of the faith.

2. The knowledge of the Son of God.

3. Maturity ("perfect man").

4. The measure of the stature of the fullness of Christ.

Christ gave the ascension gift ministries to the church so that proper church growth and development would occur. Each ministry plays an essential part in this development. To produce mature, well-balanced Christians, all five ministries must touch the individual. Spiritual maturity and unity are the goals for which we strive!

STUDY QUESTIONS

1. What is the five-fold ministry?
___
___
___
___

2. What is the purpose of the five-fold ministry?
___
___
___
___

3. What is the ministry of the apostle? prophet? evangelist? teacher? pastor?
___
___
___
___

THE CHURCH
THE MINISTRY OF THE PRESBYTERY

The ministry of the presbytery is vital in the church today. This is one way that God confirms ministry and places them in the Body of Christ. Through the laying on of hands, prophecy, and other revelation gifts, the presbyters impart spiritual gifts and confirm God's will in the lives of individuals. There is often spiritual empowerment for the person's ministry in the Body of Christ.

1.   WHAT IS THE DOCTRINE OF LAYING ON OF HANDS?

It is one of the foundational truths in the New and Old Testament (Hebrews 6:1,2). It is the belief that divine power or qualities can be transferred from one believer to another by laying hands upon another individual.

1. Throughout the Bible, the "hand" has important significance:
    a. The priest laid his hands upon the scapegoat as a means of transferring personal guilt (Leviticus 16:21,22).
    b. It is the extension of a person in the impartation of gifts:
        i. Moses imparted a portion of his wisdom and authority to Joshua (Deuteronomy 34:9).
        ii. Jesus in healing (Matthew 8:3; Mark 5:23; 7:32).
    c. It is the vehicle of blessing:
        i. Jacob placed his hands upon Joseph's children to convey blessing (Genesis 48:14-16).
        ii. Jesus bestowed His blessing upon children (Matthew 19:13-15; Mark 10:13,16).

      d. Some ways of how God chose to minister, communicate, and impart blessings to His church:
          i. Healing (Acts 28:8).
          ii. Receiving the Holy Ghost (Acts 8:17; 9:17; 19:6).
          iii. People were set apart for specific ministry (Acts 6:6; 3:2-3).
          iv. It was at times accompanied by prophecy (Acts 9:17; Acts 13:1-3; I Timothy 4:14).

2. WHO IS A PRESBYTER, AND WHAT IS A PRESBYTERY?

2. Presbyter: Any of the five-fold ministry (apostles, prophets, evangelists, pastors, and teachers) placed in the Body by God to deify and equip the saints (Ephesians 4:11,12).

3. Presbytery: A group of two or more presbyters called together by the pastor of a local church, to bring the mind and direction of the Lord into focus, when the need for such ministry is required. They are to be "seasoned" in ministry and move under the direction of the prophetic anointing.

4. WHAT IS THE PURPOSE OF PROPHECY AND LAYING ON OF HANDS AT PRESBYTERY?

The purpose of this ministry is to confirm the Lord's will for candidates and to impart empowerment for their calling. The Word of God clarifies the purpose of prophecy and the laying on of hands.

    1. Prophecy

a. A gift to individuals, which enables their ministry and placement by God to be confirmed by all (Numbers 27:18-23; Acts 13:2-4).
   b. Gift to the Body
      i. Equip believers (Ephesians 4:11,12).
      ii. Edify the Church (to strengthen and build up) (I Corinthians 14:4)
      iii. Brings direction to the church as a whole.
   c. It gives us a spiritual weapon for fighting the "good fight" (I Timothy 1:18,19; NIV).

2. Laying on of Hands
   a. Foundation stone (Hebrews 6:1,2).
   b. Point of contact for imparting something from God (Deuteronomy 34:9; I Timothy 4:14).
   c. The hands of the presbyter are used for divine and sovereign impartation from God to the candidate.

4. WHAT PREPARATION IS NEEDED FOR AN INDIVIDUAL OR CHURCH FOR THE MINISTRY OF THE PRESBYTERY?

1. A time of prayer and fasting for both the individual and the church.

2. There should be participation on the part of the church, as a whole, in maintaining the proper atmosphere of worship.

The laying on of hands with prophecy does not assure an individual a position in ministry. The individual must continually yield his vessel to God. He must also diligently study God's Word and be faithful in his service to God.

STUDY QUESTIONS

1. What is meant by "laying on of hands?"

2. Why is the hand significant?

3. What is presbytery?

4. What is prophecy?

5. How does a church prepare for presbytery?

THE CHURCH
WOMEN'S MINISTRY IN THE CHURCH

We live in the wonderful age when the promised outpouring of God's Spirit is being fulfilled. "And it shall come to pass in the last days, saith God, I will pour out my Spirit upon all flesh; and your sons and your daughters shall prophesy" (Joel 2:28,29: Acts 2:17,18). Revival, renewal, and restoration are taking place in the church today. God has promised to restore all things before the Lord Jesus comes again. One of the things God is restoring to the church today is the release of women into ministry. This has been a subject of great controversy, and two or three scriptures that have been taken out of context have hindered many. In this lesson, we will examine women's role through the Bible. By doing so, we hope to establish what the Word of God says about this issue.

1. WHAT DOES THE OLD TESTAMENT SAY ABOUT WOMEN?

1. In the Beginning, together, man and woman were to rule over the works of God's hands:

"And God said, let us make man in our image, after our likeness: and let them have dominion..."

"So God created man in His own image, in the image of God created He him; male and female created He them."

"And God blessed them, and God said unto them, be fruitful, and multiply and replenish the earth, and subdue it and have dominion..." (Genesis 1:26-28).

2. Old Testament Types and Shadows:
   a. Miriam: The Prophetess (Exodus 15:20) Here, we will note the word "prophetess" comes from the Hebrew word "Nebiah," meaning "female preacher."
   b. Deborah: Held office of prophetess and judge of the nation of Israel (Judges 4:4,5).
   c. Huldah: A Prophetess who had authority in the land and spoke forth the Word of the Lord with boldness (II Kings 22:14; II Chronicles 34:22).
   d. Esther: She had such authority that she saved the nation of Jews (Esther 2:16,17). Abigail: Wisdom to David (I Samuel 25:3-38).
   e. Abigail: A woman of good understanding, beautiful countenance, who had the spiritual insight to recognize who David was (I Samuel 25:3-38).
   f. Isaiah's Wife: A prophetess (Isaiah 8:3).
   g. Women assembled (served) at the door of the Tabernacle (Exodus 38:8).
   h. The law of the Nazarites was for women as well as men (Numbers 6:2).

3. WHAT DOES THE NEW TESTAMENT SAY ABOUT WOMEN?

1. Throughout the Gospels, Jesus restores dignity and honor to women. He, in no way, limited their opportunity to minister. Some examples are:
   a. Rebuked the apostles because they did not believe the women who were the first to see Him after He arose (Mark 16:14).
   b. Anna the Prophetess: God chose a woman to be the first person to publicly preach about Jesus after His birth (Luke 2:36-38).
   c. The Woman at the Well: Representative of an evangelist (John 4:39-42).

d. The first to see Christ resurrected were women (Matthew 28:1-10).

2. In the Book of Acts, there is no prohibition of women ministering:
   a. Priscilla: With her husband, Aquila, took Apollos and "expounded unto him the way of God more perfectly" (Acts 18:24-26).
   b. Philip had four daughters who prophesied (Acts 21:8,9).
   c. Dorcas was called a disciple (Acts 9:36).

3. In the Pauline Epistles:
   a. Phebe: a servant at the church in Cenchrea (Romans 16:1,2).

NOTE: The word servant is taken from the Greek word "diakonos." Here, it is translated as servant, but in twenty other places in the New Testament, it is translated as "minister."

4. Priscilla is again mentioned (Romans 16:3).

5. Trypena, Tryphosa, and Persis labored in the Lord (Romans 16:12).

In the 16th Chapter of Romans, Paul calls spiritual attention to these women who diligently served the Lord and ministered with Him. He did not esteem them or their work lower than his own. In Philippians, Paul also acknowledged Euodias and Syntyche as fellow workers in Christ (Philippians 4:2).

3. WHAT, THEN, DOES PAUL REFER TO IN I CORINTHIANS 14:34-36, AND I TIMOTHY 2:11,12, WHEN HE SAYS WOMEN ARE TO KEEP SILENT IN THE

CHURCH? WHAT DOES I PETER 3:7 MEAN WHEN IT REFERS TO THE WIFE AS THE "WEAKER VESSEL?"

1. In both I Corinthians and I Timothy, Paul is speaking concerning women in relationship to their husbands.
   a. I Corinthians 14:34-36: Beginning with the 11th chapter of I Corinthians, Paul gave discipline guidelines in a believer's meeting. In these particular verses, Paul was not forbidding women to minister... he was telling them not to cause confusion by "speaking out" or questioning their husbands during a church service. This was to be done at home.
   b. Timothy 2:11,12: Paul spoke of a woman in a proper relationship with her husband. Paul is not saying that the Holy Spirit cannot use a woman to minister, teach, or prophesy. He emphasizes that a woman cannot have dominion over or assume a place of authority above that of her husband. True ministry will flow only as divine order is established in the home.

2. I Peter 3:7: This, again, deals with a husband/wife relationship. The word "weaker" carries the connotation of one lesser in authority. Not all women are to be weaker vessels than all men. Married women are considered the weaker vessels (or ones in lesser authority) in the home and marriage relationship. In the home, God has set a line of authority: First God, then Christ, next the man, then the woman (I Corinthians 11:3). In the marriage relationship, the wife is to be the weaker vessel. But before God, she and her husband are heirs together of the grace of life (I Peter 3:7).

3. Paul recognized that the church ("ekklesia") did not refer to a building but rather a people (both male and female) that have obeyed the Word of God to come out from amongst the worlds. Galatians 3:26-29 tells us who this church is:
   a. "For ye are all the children of God by faith in Christ Jesus."
   b. "For as many of you as have been baptized into Christ have put on Christ."
   c. "There is neither Jew nor Greek, there is neither bond nor free, there is neither male nor female: For ye are all one in Christ Jesus."
   d. "And if ye be Christ's, then ye are Abraham's seed, and heirs according to the promise."

A study of these scriptures and their meanings makes it evident that Paul was not saying that women could not minister in the church. He was saying that wives should not be a disturbance to the ministry of the Holy Spirit. He was not saying that a woman cannot teach the Word of God or proclaim the Good News, but Paul did say that the woman could not have dominion over her husband, nor could she teach such.

STUDY QUESTIONS

1. What significance does Joel 2:28,29 have on women?
_____
_____
_____
_____

2. How were women used by God in Old Testament times?
_____
_____
_____
_____

3.	Cite Biblical examples of women being used in the New Testament:
_____
_____
_____

4.	How do you understand I Corinthians 14:34-36 and I Timothy 2:11,12?
_____
_____
_____
_____

KINGDOM LIVING
KINGDOM OF GOD

The Kingdom of God is eternal, an everlasting kingdom where Jesus rules and reigns as King. It is established in the believer's heart as he surrenders his all to the Lordship of Jesus. It is the rule of God in the hearts, minds, and wills of His people. Though it is a Kingdom ordained before all other kingdoms, it will remain after all other kingdoms crumble and fall - the Kingdom of God is now at hand!

1. **WHAT IS THE KINGDOM OF GOD?**

    1. It is a condition - the rule of God in the lives of His people (Colossians 1:13; Luke 17:21).

    2. It is an everlasting Kingdom (Daniel 4:3; II Peter 1:11; Luke 1:33).

    3. It is superior to, and above, all kingdoms (Psalm 103:19).

    4. It is not of the world (John 18:36).

    5. It is righteousness, peace, and joy in the Holy Ghost (Romans 14:17).

    6. Not only in word but in power (I Corinthians 4:20).

2. **HOW DO WE RECEIVE KINGDOM CITIZENSHIP?**

    1. By the right of creatorship (Genesis 1:27,28). From the beginning of time, God intended to endow mankind with authority over all creation. Man was created in the image of God and created to rule and reign with Him.

    2. By right of inheritance as believers (Matthew 25:34).

     a. Must be born again to receive (John 3:1-5).
     b. Not to be inherited by flesh and blood (I Corinthians 15:50).
     c. We are to seek it above all else (Matthew 6:33).

3. WHAT IS OUR COMMISSION IN THE KINGDOM?

Matthew 28:18-20 And Jesus came and spake unto them, saying, "All power is given unto me in heaven and earth. Go ye therefore, and teach all nations, baptizing them in the name of the Father, and the Son and the Holy Ghost: Teaching them to observe whatsoever I have commanded you: and Lo, I am with you always, even unto the end of the world. Amen."

4. WHAT CHARACTERISTICS ARE MANIFESTED IN KINGDOM CITIZENS?

1. A change in CHARACTER (Matthew 5:3,4,6,8; I Peter 1:14-16; Romans 12:2).

2. A change in CONDUCT (Matthew 5:5,7,9; I Timothy 4:12).

3. We become an INFLUENCE on the world in which we live (Matthew 5:13-16). The Kingdom is within the believer's heart. This is where God wants to reign, even as He does in heaven (Matthew 6:10). He also desires that we receive the benefits that are ours as Kingdom citizens: righteousness, peace, and joy! (Romans 14:17).

STUDY QUESTIONS

1. What is the Kingdom of God?
   _____
   _____
   _____

2. Who is the King?
   _____
   _____
   _____

3. Who are "Kingdom Citizens?"
   _____
   _____
   _____

4. When is God's Kingdom established?
   _____
   _____
   _____

KINGDOM LIVING
RESURRECTION OF THE DEAD AND ETERNAL JUDGEMENT

Hebrews 6:1,2 lists six basic foundational truths; among these is the resurrection of the dead and eternal judgment. Belief in the resurrection is necessary to provide an adequate foundation in the believer's life. Faith in a resurrected Lord gives meaning to our existence in the Kingdom. It is the basis of our present and future hope (I Corinthians 15:12-17).

1. WHAT ARE THE RESURRECTIONS THAT THE NEW TESTAMENT BELIEVER MUST CONSIDER?

1. Past: Of Jesus Christ.

2. Present: Spiritual resurrection of the believer (Colossians 2:12,13; Romans 6:4-7).

3. Future: Final resurrection of "all that are in the grave."

2. DID JESUS ACTUALLY RISE FROM THE DEAD?

1. Yes. The Old and New Testaments substantiate this (Psalms 16:8-11; 110:1; Matthew 28:6; Act 3:15).

2. Jesus was seen after His resurrection (I Corinthians 15:5-8; Luke 24:13-35; John 20:18-20).

3. Jesus was resurrected with the same body that was crucified (John 2:19-22; Luke 24:36-40; John 20:27,28).

3. WHAT IS DECLARED IN THE RESURRECTION OF JESUS CHRIST?

1. Justification (Romans 4:25; 5:1, II Corinthians 5:15).

2. Death is defeated (Romans 6:9; I Corinthians 15:54-58)

3. Jesus is the Son of God (Romans 1:4).

4. Jesus is Lord of all (Ephesians 1:20-23; Colossians 1:16-20).

5. A new life source (I Peter 1:3).

4. **HOW ARE WE PRESENTLY RESURRECTED?**

1. It is expressed through water baptism (Romans 6:4,5; Colossians 2:12,13).

2. We are quickened or "made alive together in Christ" (Ephesians 2:1; 4-6; II Corinthians 5:15; Romans 6:8).

3. Our lives reflect the change:
    a. We serve a new master (II Corinthians 5:15; Romans 6:18).
    b. We have a new life (Romans 6:4; 7:6; Ephesians 4:22-24).
    c. We have a new purpose (Colossians 3:1,2; Romans 8:28).

5. **WHAT DOES THE BIBLE SAY ABOUT THE FUTURE RESURRECTION?**

1. Only God knows when it will occur (I Thessalonians 4:16,17; John 6:39,40,44,54).

2. All that are in the grave shall be resurrected (Acts 24:15).

3. We shall receive a glorious body (Philippians 3:21; I John 3:2; I Corinthians 15:29,38,49).

6. **WHAT IS MEANT BY ETERNAL JUDGMENT?**

Judgment means the "result of judging, trying or passing sentence upon; judicial decision." Eternal does not only mean everlasting but also a "final, or that which has no appeal."

7. **WHY MUST THERE BE A JUDGMENT?**

    1. Ungodliness (Jude 15; II Peter 2:6-9).

    2. Disobedience (Romans 2:6-11; Jude 6; Hebrews 3:18).

    3. Unbelief (John 3:18; Acts 4:12; John 5:24).

    4. Sin (Romans 5:12; I Corinthians 15:21,22).

8. **WHO WILL JUDGE AND HOW?**

    1. God: The judge of all (Hebrews 12:23).

    2. God's throne has been established for judgment (Psalms 9:7,8).

    3. Will be administered by Christ:
        a. The Father has committed all judgment and given the authority to judge to the Son (John 5:22,27).
        b. Jesus was ordained to be the judge (Acts 10:42).
        c. Jesus will sit in the judgment seat (Romans 14:10-13).

9. **WHEN WILL JUDGMENT TAKE PLACE?**

Like the resurrection, eternal judgment has three aspects:

    1. Past:

a. Sin (Isaiah 53:4-6; Hebrews 10:1-14; John 1:29).
  b. Satan (John 16:11; Colossians 2:15).
  c. Man (John 3:18; 5:24; Romans 5:9; 8:1).

2. Present:
  a. Sinners (Romans 1:18-31; Ephesians 5:6).
  b. Believers (I Corinthians 11:31,32; I Timothy 1:20; Hebrews 12:8-10).

3. Future:
  a. Believers: Judged for their works and rewarded (Revelation 11:18; Matthew 25:31-46; I Corinthians 3:11-15; 4:5).
  b. Sinners: Judged for their sin and disobedience and punished (II Thessalonians 1:8,9; Revelation 20:15).

10. WHEN WILL THIS FUTURE JUDGMENT TAKE PLACE?

1. After death (Hebrews 9:27).

2. The last day (John 12:48).

3. The "Day of Judgement" (Matthew 10:15; I John 4:17; II Peter 2:9).

4. The Second Coming (Matthew 25:31; II Thessalonians 1:7-10; II Timothy 4:1).

11. WHAT DOES THE CERTAINTY OF JUDGMENT PRODUCE?

1. A Motive for repentance (Acts 17:31,32).

2. Holiness (II Corinthians 5:9; II Peter 3:11,14).

3. Prayer and watchfulness (Mark 13:33).

4. Keep us from judging one another (Romans 14:10-14).

Because Christ was raised from the dead, our faith is not in vain, and we receive salvation from our sins. It is His life that gives life and shall yet quicken the dead!

STUDY QUESTIONS

1. How many resurrections does the Bible mention?

_____
_____
_____
_____

2. What does the believer receive through Jesus' resurrection?

_____
_____
_____
_____

3. What is "eternal judgment?"

_____
_____
_____
_____

4. Who will be judged? By Whom?

_____
_____
_____
_____

KINGDOM LIVING
CHRISTIAN HOME AND FAMILY

As God is bringing restoration and order to the Household of God (the Church), we find that the home plays a vital part in this visitation. In the Old Testament, the family was the corporate body of worshipers, with the Father as the spiritual leader and authority (Joshua 24:15).

1. HOW IS THE CHRISTIAN HOME ESTABLISHED?

A material house does not come together without a blueprint. As Christians, the blueprint of God's Word is our guideline for establishing our home.

1. Every institution must have a proper foundation (Matthew 7:24-27; Luke 6:46-49).
    a. The proper foundation for the family unit is first to be "born again."
    b. Not only hear the Word of God but also practice it as it relates to the family unit and relationships within the family.

2. A home must be built (Psalm 127:1; Proverbs 14:1).
    a. Each member has a responsibility.
    b. As each member functions in his/her area of responsibility, the home will be built.

3. Divinely instituted government must be within the home (Ephesians 6:1-4; 5:22-32). There is a "chain of command" within the home, even as there is in the Church or civil government. (Jesus, Father, Mother, Children) (I Corinthians 11:3; Colossians 1:18).

2. **WHAT IS THE PURPOSE OF HEADSHIP?**

   1. The Scriptures declare that the husband and wife are "one flesh. "Thus, headship is not intended to bring about division but unity.

   2. Headship does not mean:
      a. Dictatorship.
      b. Inequality of men, women, or children.
      c. Inferiority of women.
      d. Superiority of men.

3. **WHAT IS MARRIAGE?**

   1. Covenants are publicly made between a man and a woman, and God, to found and maintain a family.

   2. Of vital interest to God. He instituted it in (Genesis 1:26-28, and 2:18-25).

   3. It is intended to be a life-long union that can only be dissolved by death (Romans 7:2,3) or unfaithfulness. Matthew 19:6 says, "Wherefore they are no more twain, but one flesh. What therefore God hath joined together, let no man put asunder."

4. **WHAT ARE THE RESPONSIBILITIES OF THE HUSBAND AND WIFE?**

   1. Husband:
      a. He must acknowledge and confess Jesus Christ as Lord of his life.
      b. He must accept that God has ordained that he be the head of his household (Ephesians 5:23, 24) and

that he himself is under headship (I Corinthians 11:3).
- c. He must recognize that God created his wife to be his help meet, not help-mate (Genesis 2:18).
- d. He must recognize that his wife is of like nature and substance (Genesis 2:23).
  - a. He must leave his father and mother and cleave to his wife (Ephesians 5:31).
  - b. He must recognize that he and his wife are one, even as Christ and the Church are one (Ephesians 5:30,31).
  - c. He must love his wife as Christ loved the Church (Ephesians 5:2; 25-31).
  - d. He must sacrifice for his wife; give himself even as Christ gave Himself for the church (Ephesians 5:25).
  - e. He must nourish ("to promote health and strength to") his wife (Ephesians 5:29).
  - f. He must cherish ("to impart warmth, foster, care for") his wife (Ephesians 5:29).

2. Wife:
   - a. She must know her area of responsibility. Husband and wife are equal as persons but not equal in responsibility.
   - b. Must accept responsibility with the right attitude. The woman is not inferior to man; nor competing with man.
   - c. She must have a submissive spirit (Hebrew meaning: "to come under the protection of another") (Ephesians 5:22-24; Colossians 3:18; I Peter 3:1-6)
   - d. She must have a quiet and meek spirit (I Peter 3:1-6).
   - e. She must be modest and Godly (I Timothy 3:9,10).

- f. Recognize that she and her husband are heirs together of the grace of life (I Peter 3:7).
- g. The wife is the helpmeet, the complement to her husband (Genesis 2:18).
- h. She is to love her husband and children (Titus 2:4).

A marriage must pivot around God's will and God's purpose for their lives. When a couple is married, they begin the adventure of "oneness." It can only be encountered as they both love God and one another. They cannot follow two independent courses of action.

5. WHAT DOES THE BIBLE SAY ABOUT CHILDREN?

1. They are the heritage of the Lord (Psalms 127:3-5).

2. They are the reward of the Lord (Psalms 127:3; 113:9; Genesis 33:5).

3. God highly esteemed them (Psalms 127:4,5; 128:3; Matthew 19:14).

4. They are a crown (Proverbs 17:6).

6. WHAT ARE THE SCRIPTURAL RESPONSIBILITIES OF PARENTS?

1. They must bring their children to Jesus Christ (Matthew 19:13,14; Mark 10:13).

2. Parents must:
   - a. Love God.
   - b. Study His Word.
   - c. Teach their children to do the same (Deuteronomy 6:5-7).

3. Parents must administer correction when needed:
    a. Correction is an act of love (Proverbs 13:24).
    b. Correction will drive out foolishness (Proverbs 22:15).
        i. Foolishness, if not corrected, will produce pride (Proverbs 14:3).
        ii. Foolishness and pride yield:
    c. Contention (Proverbs 13:10).
    d. Strife (Proverbs 28:25).
    e. Shame (Proverbs 11:2, 29:15)
    f. Withholding correction will destroy a child (Proverbs 23:13,14).

4. Parents are to train their children (Proverbs 22:6).

5. Definition of train: "to bring to a requisite standard, as of conduct of skill, by practiced and careful instruction; specifically, to mold the character of; educate; instruct; to render skillful or proficient."

6. Parents are not to provoke their children but bring them up in the nature and admonition of the Lord (Ephesians 6:4; Colossians 3:21).

7. **WHAT ARE THE RESPONSIBILITIES OF THE CHILD TOWARD HIS PARENTS?**

1. Children are to honor their parents (Deuteronomy 5:16; Ephesians 6:2,3).

2. The Christian home provides the foundation for the Church. Our relationships with family members teach us principles vital to building strong relationships with God and His body. Through the family, we learn to love, serve, and tenderly care for one another.

STUDY QUESTIONS

1. What is marriage?
   _____
   _____
   _____
   _____

2. What are the husband's responsibilities to his wife?
   _____
   _____
   _____
   _____

3. What are the wife's responsibilities to her husband?
   _____
   _____
   _____
   _____

4. What does God's Word say about children?
   _____
   _____
   _____
   _____

5. What are parents' responsibilities to their children?
   _____
   _____
   _____

KINGDOM LIVING
EVANGELISM

The theme of soul-winning is predominated throughout the history of the Church. It is the life-flow of the assembly. II Corinthians 5:18-20 expresses both our commission to evangelize and the importance of fulfilling this commission to evangelize and the importance of fulfilling this commission: "And all things are of God, who hath reconciled us to Himself by Jesus Christ, and hath given to us the ministry of reconciliation; To wit, that God was in Christ, reconciling the world unto Himself, not imputing their trespasses unto them; and hath committed unto us the word of reconciliation. Now then we are ambassadors for Christ, as though God did beseech you by us; we pray you in Christ's stead, be ye reconciled to God." (II Corinthians 5:18-20)

1. WHAT DOES IT MEAN TO BE AN "AMBASSADOR" FOR CHRIST?

We are to be evangelists or those who proclaim or announce the Gospel or "good news."

1. Personal evangelism speaks of the Biblical responsibility of reproduction:
    a. God created all living things with the ability to reproduce (Genesis 1:12,21,22,28).
    b. God intended that every living thing bring forth its own kind (Genesis 1:11,12).
    c. This principle holds true in the Kingdom of God (John 15:16; Romans 7:4).

2. It is the purpose and will of God that we (the Church) proclaim the good news:
    a. Jesus called Peter to be a "fisher of men" (Matthew 4:19).

- b. Jesus commissioned the disciples to teach all nations (Matthew 28:18-20).
- c. Jesus desired the gospel to be preached to every creature (Mark 16:15,16).
- d. Repentance and remission of sins should be preached to all nations (Luke 24:47,48).

2. **IS THE "GOOD NEWS" IMPERATIVE? YES, because:**

1. The first Adam, through rebellion, fell into sin and lost fellowship with God. We are born into the image of the first Adam and therefore, every person in the world is born in sin and knows rebellion towards God (Psalms 51:1-19; Romans 2:9-12; 5:12-21).

2. All are dead in trespasses and sin (Ephesians 2:1).

3. The unbeliever, by nature, is a child of wrath (Ephesians 2:3).

4. All are estranged from the Life of God (Ephesians 4:18).

5. All are under condemnation (Romans 3:19).

3. **WHAT IS THE "GOOD NEWS?"**

The "good news" is expressed in several different ways throughout the Bible. It begins with God as the initiator in restoring man to fellowship with Himself. John 3:16 states, "For God so loved the world..."

1. God became a man (Philippians 2:5-8).

2. Jesus was also the express image of God (Hebrews 1:3; II Corinthians 4:4; Colossians 1:15).

3. Jesus did not sin as Adam did (Hebrews 4:15; II Corinthians 5:21; Hebrews 7:26).

4. The Lord Jesus received and paid the penalty of sin (Galatians 2:20; Romans 4:25; 5:6,8; 8:32; Ephesians 5:2).

THEREFORE...

5. Every person who receives, accepts, and acknowledges Jesus Christ as their Lord and Savior, accepts the finished work of Calvary as their only means of salvation and repents of their sins, is born into Christ (John 3:1-5; 14:6; Acts 2:38,39).

6. In Jesus Christ:
    a. We are made righteous (Romans 4:5, 22-25; II Corinthians 5:21).
    b. There is no condemnation (Romans 8:1,2,34).
    c. We are conformed to the very image of God (Romans 8:28-30; I Corinthians 15:49; Colossians 3:10).
    d. We are brought to peace with God (Romans 5:1).
    e. We receive access to the Father (Romans 5:2; Ephesians 2:18; 3:12).
    f. We are restored to full fellowship with God (Ephesians 1:18; Colossians 1:27; Romans 8:15-17).

4. WHO HAS THE RESPONSIBILITY TO PROCLAIM THE "GOOD NEWS?"

1. Man cannot discover a means of salvation apart from a revelation of God through the preaching of the Word of God (Romans 10:17,18; 16:25,26).

2. The proclamation of the gospel has been given to the church as a whole (Matthew 28:18-20; Ephesians 3:9-11).

3. The gospel's message is to be delivered by all believers as individuals (Mark 16:15-20; Acts 1:8).

4. The importance of this commission is supported throughout the Bible:
    a. Jesus' ministry was evangelistic (Matthew 11:5; Luke 4:18, 43; 8:1).
    b. Jesus sent out evangelistic ministry (Luke 9:6).
    c. Paul was prepared to teach the gospel everywhere (Romans 1:5).
    d. The early church was involved in evangelism (Acts 8:4,12,25,35,40; 13:1-5,32; 14:7,21).
    e. We are admonished to share the "good news" (Romans 10:12-18; I Corinthians 9:16,1
    f. He that wins souls is wise (Proverbs 11:30).

As we "let our light so shine before men," we should be ready, at any given moment, to share the gospel with anyone who may ask us the reason for our hope (I Peter 3:15).

STUDY QUESTIONS

1.   What is an "ambassador" for Christ?

_____
_____
_____
_____

2.   What is the "Good News"?

_____
_____
_____
_____

3. What does Proverbs 11:30 tell us?

4. What importance does the Bible place on evangelism?

KINGDOM LIVING
POSSESSION

There is much teaching today along the lines of demon possession of Christians. This very dangerous teaching can and has hindered many believers in their walk with the Lord. It is for this reason that we have felt it necessary to include a correct teaching on this subject.

1. **WHAT DOES IT MEAN TO BE "POSSESSED?"**

    1. According to Webster's Dictionary, being possessed means "to be influenced or controlled by a demon". The word possess means: "to have as property; to own. "It comes from the Latin word "possidere," which means "to sit as master."

    2. We can see from the meaning of the word itself that we are owned, influenced, or controlled in all we do by the one who possesses us.

2. **NOW THE QUESTION IS "WHO OWNS US?"**

    1. The Word of God says that we, as Christians, have been bought with a price (I Corinthians 6:20).

    2. This "buying back" is more commonly referred to as redemption.
        a. Redemption is "the action of recovering ownership by paying a specified sum."
        b. The price, or specified sum, was the blood of Jesus Christ (Acts 20:28; I Peter 1:18,19; Revelation 5:9).

    3. Before being redeemed, we are sold into the bondage of sin (Romans 7:14) and are walking according to the prince of the power of the air, the devil (Ephesians 2:2).

3. **CAN WE HAVE TWO OWNERS OR MASTERS?**

   1. The Bible clearly states that there is no neutrality.
      a. You are either for Christ or against Him (Matthew 12:30).
      b. You will either serve sin or serve righteousness (Romans 6:16).
      c. You cannot serve two masters (Matthew 6:24).

   2. The Bible also tells us that we, individually and collectively, are the temple of God (I Corinthian 3:16,17). We can draw an interesting parallel between our subject and the account in I Samuel 5:1-5. The ark of God was brought into the house of a pagan god, Dagon. This god was unable to stand in the presence of God without being destroyed.

4. **ARE THERE ANY SCRIPTURAL REFERENCES TO SUPPORT THE TEACHING THAT CHRISTIANS CAN BE POSSESSED BY A DEMON?**

   1. There is none. In all cases, those who had demons cast out of them were not saved or "born again."

   2. The Spirit of the Lord is far more powerful than that of the devil.
      a. Jesus exercised authority over demons and unclean spirits:
         i. A devil cast out of a dumb demoniac (Matthew 9:33).
         ii. Unclean spirit cast out (Mark 1:23-27).
         iii. Demoniac of Gadara healed (Mark 5:1-19).
         iv. Seven devils cast out of Mary Magdalene (Luke 8:2).

      b. Apostles had authority over unclean spirits and demons:
          i. Jesus gives the apostles power against unclean spirits and the power to cast them out.
          ii. (Matthew 10:1).
          iii. Apostles healed everyone...those vexed with unclean spirits (Acts 5:16).
          iv. Paul commanded the evil spirit to come out of a damsel (Acts 16:18).
          v. Again, speaks of Paul as having authority over evil spirits (Acts 19:12).
      c. This power and authority are imparted to us as believers (Mark 16:14-20).

3. We are called God's "peculiar people." This does not mean that we are odd or strange, but that we are "a people for God's own possession" or His "special treasure" (I Peter 2:9).

5. CAN WE HAVE CONFIDENCE THAT WE WILL REMAIN GOD'S POSSESSION? - YES!

1. No one can snatch us out of His hand (John 10:28,29).

2. We are told that those whom the Son sets free are free indeed (John 8:36).

As we continually allow God to fill us with His Holy Spirit, we find no longer room for another spirit to reside within us. Webster's Dictionary states that when something is full or filled, there is room for nothing else. Paul, in Ephesians 4:27, tells us not to give place to the devil, and in James 4:7, we find: "Submit yourselves therefore to God. Resist the devil, and he will flee from you." As we submit our vessels to be filled with

God's Holy Spirit, the devil, and his demons will flee from our very presence. There is no room for them to reside in our beings.

STUDY QUESTIONS

1. What does "possession" mean?
   _____
   _____
   _____
   _____

2. What does "redemption" mean?
   _____
   _____
   _____
   _____

3. Who has ownership rights to the believer?
   _____
   _____
   _____
   _____

4. What does Mark 16:14-20 promise the believer?
   _____
   _____
   _____
   _____

KINGDOM LIVING
RESPONSIBILITY OF CHRISTIAN CITIZENSHIP

Christians have dual citizenship. We are citizens of the Kingdom of God, seated with Christ now in the heavenlies (Ephesians 2:6), yet we also dwell in this world. It is our responsibility to influence others for our King. Therefore, the Christian must not only minister within the walls of the Church but must impact the community, marketplace, and nations.

1. WHAT SHOULD BE OUR RELATIONSHIP TO THIS WORLD? WE ARE:

1. Commanded to be in the world but not of it (John 17:14-18).

2. Not to love the world (I John 2:15) nor to conform to the world (Romans 12:1-2).

3. To take dominion (Genesis 1:26; I John 5:2-5).

4. To be salt and light (Matthew 5:13-16).

5. To be ambassadors for Christ and instruments for His mercy and blessing (II Corinthians 5:20).

2. HOW SHOULD WE CONDUCT OURSELVES?

1. With integrity (Proverbs 11:3; Proverbs 20:7).

2. With excellence, as if our work is for the Lord (Colossians 3:23).

3. With wisdom (Matthew 10:16).

4. Holding worldly goods loosely (Mark 8:36).

3. **SHOULD A CHRISTIAN PARTICIPATE IN POLITICS?**

   1. Whether one realizes it or not, Christians are a part of the political system. Lethargy and inactivity are negative involvements that promote the ascendancy and rule of evil men (Psalms 125:3; Proverbs 12:24).

   2. We extend Christian influence by participating. Christians should assert their influence in organizations that are part of their daily lives (Genesis 41:33).

   3. Only Christians are equipped spiritually and morally to render the kind of political decisions that will be pleasing to God (Proverbs 14:34; II Chronicles 7:14).

4. **HOW DOES A CHRISTIAN PARTICIPATE IN POLITICS?**

   1. Pray.
      a. ...that the Spirit of God will enable you to live a Godly life and introduce others to Christ - the first step to good citizenship (I Timothy 2:1,2).
      b. ...that God will remove from office those disobedient to Him so that righteous rule will be restored, and America will turn from her wicked ways. Remember that Godless rulership is contagious (Proverbs 29:12).
      c. ...that men and women of God will be elected to public office at all levels of leadership so that our land will be healed (Psalms 33:12).

   2. Register to vote and vote!

Many of God's people throughout America are not even registered to vote. Only when you have registered to vote will you be able to help elect Godly officials (Proverbs 11:11).

3. Help elect Godly People.

Help elect men and women of God to public office and support them faithfully throughout their terms (Proverbs 29:2). The Word of God gives us the basic qualifications of a good candidate (Exodus 18:21,22):

    a. Godliness.
    b. Integrity.
    c. Industry.
    d. Biblical guidance.
    e. Justice.
    f. Demonstrated capability (competence in managing business or professional affairs).

4. Remember that principles are more important than party. Vote your Christian convictions in preference to your party. To place confidence in unworthy candidates merely because of political party is a miscarriage of Christian stewardship (Proverbs 15:19).

5. WHAT ARE OTHER AREAS OF SPECIAL INFLUENCE FOR OUR CHRISTIAN WITNESS?

1. Business world (our workplace).

2. Neighborhood and community.

3. Educational systems

4. Communications and the arts.

STUDY QUESTIONS

1. What should be our relationship to this world?
___
___
___
___

2. How should we conduct ourselves in the world?
___
___
___
___

3. Should Christians have a voice in politics?
___
___
___
___

4. How can we participate in politics?
___
___
___
___

KINGDOM LIVING
RESPONSIBILITIES OF THE COVENANT COMMUNITY

So then, "As you received Christ Jesus the Lord, walk in Him, having been rooted and being built up in Him, and being confirmed in the faith just as you were taught" (Colossians 2:6,7). The hope and prayer of the ministry is that having come this far, each of you has allowed your life to be deeply rooted and established in Christ and He in you. The absence of this accomplished work in our lives only spells unnecessary trouble. Our objective and goal are to grow up to mature, both individually and collectively, as we make up a small part of the Body of Christ. Growth and development are accomplished through various means (The Word, the Spirit, the Ministry, and the Right relationship to others in the Body). But whether alone or together, God requires faithfulness to the added responsibilities, which go hand-in-hand with maturity. As we have entered into a covenant relationship with God, we find ourselves committed not only to Him but also to all those who make up His Body. In such a relationship, the depth of our maturity is tested, and we stand accountable to God for our faithfulness to such a relationship.

1.   RESPONSIBILITIES OF THE PASTORS (UNDER SHEPHERDS).

1. Preach Christ (I Corinthians 1:23; Acts 8:5; 10:36; 17:3).

2. Teach the Word (Matthew 28:20; I Timothy 3:2; 4:11; II Timothy 2:25).

3. Feed and nourish the flock (John 21:17; Acts 20:28; I Peter 5:2).

4. Prepare the body for the work of the ministry (Ephesians 4:12).

5. Spiritual watchmen over the flock:
    a. Protect against false teaching (Acts 20:28-30).
    b. Discipline individuals or the body as a whole (I Thessalonians 5:14).
    c. Govern and lead people according to God's Word.
    d. As part of this responsibility, the pastors have drawn up the following guidelines as a means of knowing those who labor among us:
        i. Each person is expected to faithfully and regularly attend Covenant Life Church services.
        ii. Each person must have completed at least eight "First Principles" classes.
        iii. Must be baptized in water.
        iv. Must be filled with the Baptism of the Holy Spirit or actively seeking it.
        v. Is expected, at all times, to have a good witness in their personal lives, such as:
        vi. Dress in moderation (mini-skirts and shorts are not considered appropriate attire for women or men while functioning in any church ministry). Modesty is a must among church leaders.
        vii. "Let no corrupt communication proceed out of your mouth, but that which is good to the use of edifying that it may minister grace unto the hearers" (Ephesians 4:29).
        viii. Is asked to seek the Lord and be in good spirit and attitude when ministering to others.

If one feels they can meet the stated requirements, after prayerfully considering these guidelines, their involvement must be one of their priorities.

2. **RESPONSIBILITIES OF THE FLOCK.**

   1. To the Pastors:
      a. Prayer support (Romans 15:30).
      b. Honor, respect, and love (Philippians 2:29; I Thessalonians 5:12,13).
      c. Monetary support (I Corinthians 9:6-14; Galatians 6:6; I Timothy 5:17,18).
      d. Obey and submit to them (Hebrews 13:17).

   2. To fellow members of the body:
      a. Ministering spiritual abilities (I Corinthians 14:26; I Peter 4:10).
      b. Prayer and intercession (Ephesians 6:18; II Corinthians 1:11).
      c. Love (Colossians 2:2; Hebrews 13:1; I Peter 2:17).
      d. Comfort (I Thessalonians 4:18; 5:11; II Corinthians 1:4).
      e. Hospitality (I Peter 4:9; Romans 12:13; Hebrews 13:2).
      f. Time and strength (Galatians 66:10; Proverbs 3:27).
      g. Money and possessions (Romans 12:13; I John 3:17).

3. **DISCERNING THE BODY**

   1. One body with many members (Romans 12:5; I Corinthians 12:12).

   2. Each member is placed in the body by God (I Corinthians 12:18).

   3. The Holy Spirit gives Gifts (not earned) for the good of all (I Corinthians 12:4-11). These differ in:

KIND	PURPOSE	RESULTS

APPENDICES
CONFIRMATION

Confirmation is a sacrament that was instituted by Christ through His disciples. Through confirmation, believers receive strength and become established in Jesus Christ. It is a time when those who have been faithful to attend and to submit to the teachings of a local assembly receive both human and divine approval.

1. WHAT DOES THE WORD "CONFIRMATION" MEAN?

It means "to make secure; to stabilize; to establish; to make firm; to render constant and unwavering."

2. WAS CONFIRMATION PRACTICED IN NEW TESTAMENT TIMES? - YES!

1. The Apostles confirmed their converts after their initial experiences with Christ.

2. The Apostles confirmed after times of teaching (Acts 14;21,22).

3. Confirmation includes being challenged and exhorted to go on in what we have learned (Acts 15:32).

4. At times, they confirmed a whole church (Acts 15:40,41).

3. WHY IS CONFIRMATION NECESSARY?

1. Prepares believers to stand during times of testing (Luke 8:13-15).

2. Grounds the believer against deception (Ephesians 4:14).

3. Motivates the believer to continually appropriate present-day truths (II Peter 1:10,12).

4. **WHAT RESULTS WILL CONFIRMATION PRODUCE?**

   1. Produces individuals whose hearts are established in faith and grace.

   2. Hearts established in holiness are free to love one another (I Thessalonians 3:12,13).

   3. Enrichment in all knowledge by Christ (I Corinthians 1:5,6).

   4. Walk worthily, with joy, through all we may encounter (Colossians 1:10,11).

   5. The believer becomes equipped to live above reproach (Colossians 1:22,23).

   6. Makes believers thankful (Colossians 2:6,7).

   7. Without confirmation, the church is weak. Young Christians must be firmly established in the truth, or they will become discouraged and often fall. During testing, believers who can endure the chastening of the Lord are candidates to become mature sons of God.

COVENANT LIFE WORSHIP CENTER - COVENANT OF CONFIRMATION

MINISTRY: We, the ministry of this church, desire to make a covenant with you as faithful members of this local assembly and the Body of Christ.

Will you pledge to be faithful in attending church services as stated in Hebrews 10:25? ("Not forsaking the assembling of ourselves together, as the manner of some is but exhorting one another: and so much the more as ye see the day approaching").

CLASS: I will.

MINISTRY: Will you be diligent in studying the Word of God as written in II Timothy 2:15? ("Study to shew thyself approved unto God, a workman that needeth not to be ashamed, rightly dividing the word of truth").

CLASS: I will.

MINISTRY: Will you faithfully pray for this ministry and those in the leadership of our nation, following I Timothy 2:1,2? ("I exhort therefore, that first of all, supplications; prayer; intercessions; and giving of thanks; be made for all men; for Kings and for all that are in authority: that we may lead a quiet and peaceable life in all godliness and honesty").

CLASS: I will.

MINISTRY: Will you always conduct your life to the glory of God, patterning your life after Christ? I John 2:6: ("He that saith he abideth in Him ought himself also so to walk, even as He walked").

CLASS: I will.

MINISTRY: Will you be faithful in giving tithes and offerings as found in Malachi 3:10, so that there might be bread in the house of the Lord? ("Bring ye all the tithes into the storehouse, that there may be meat in mine house and prove Me now wherewith saith the Lord of Hosts, if I will not open you the windows of heaven and pour you out a blessing that there shall not be room enough to receive it").

CLASS: I will.

MINISTRY: In turn, we, the ministry of this church, pledge to feed you as God's flock according to I Peter 5:2,3: ("Feed the flock of God, which is among you, taking the oversight thereof, not by constraint, but willingly: not for filthy lucre, but of a ready mind. Neither as being lords over God's heritage but being examples to the flock").

We will teach you in the ways of the Lord; in the Word; Spirit; and in counsel as Paul exhorted Timothy in II Timothy 2:2: ("And the things that thou hast heard of me among many witnesses, the same commit thou to faithful men, who shall be able to teach others also").

And, we will watch over your souls so at the day of His coming that we might be able to give a good account for your life here on earth as found in Hebrews 13:17: ("Obey them that have the rule over you and submit yourselves: for they watch for your souls as they that must give account, that they may do it with joy, and not with grief: for that is unprofitable for you").

PERSONAL WITNESS:
PART I

During this current wave of revival flooding our country and the world, many varied approaches, and tools for "personal evangelism" have emerged. There are cartoon-illustrated tracts, fill-in-the-blank spiritual inventory cards, cleverly diagramed salvation plans, comic books, etc. The list is endless, but the objective is to bring sinners to a saving knowledge of Jesus Christ. The news media splashes exhilarating statistics concerning the number of people who claim a "born-again" experience in print and on the airwaves. But what about unpublished, seldom-mentioned statistics concerning those whose experience has been short-lived and fizzled out!? Salvation is more than simple agreement or assent to the claims of Jesus Christ. It is a total commitment, a changed life (II Corinthians 5:17). Weak converts, who are not established in God according to the Biblical pattern, too soon revert to sin and slide back into the world. Our task, therefore, is to lead sinners into a full salvation experience and get them established in the Kingdom of God.

1. JESUS HAS COMMANDED US TO SPREAD THIS GOSPEL OF THE KINGDOM.

   1. Matthew 28:19,20.

   2. Mark 16:15,16.

   3. Luke 24:47,48.

2. **WHAT EXACTLY IS THE MESSAGE WE ARE TO SHARE?**

   1. "... what must I do to be saved? ... Believe on the Lord Jesus Christ and thou shalt be saved... they spake unto him the Word of the Lord ... and was baptized, he and all his, straightway" (Acts 16:30-33).

   2. "... what shall we do?" Then Peter said unto them, "repent and be baptized every one of you in the Name of Jesus Christ for the remission of sins and ye shall receive the gift of the Holy Ghost" (Acts 2:37,38).

3. **TRUE CONVICTION GOES BEYOND A SIMPLE "BORN-AGAIN" EXPERIENCE.**

   1. "Except a man be born again, he cannot see the Kingdom of God" (John 3:3).

   2. "Except a man be born of water and of the Spirit, he cannot enter into the Kingdom of God" (John 3:5).

   3. Throughout Scripture, there is indeed a pattern where multiple experiences, witnesses, or occurrences are used to validate and confirm His will and be established in His Kingdom. God has set a multiplicity pattern throughout scripture to establish any word or matter.
      a. "... at the mouth of two witnesses, or at the mouth of three witnesses, shall the matter be established" (Deuteronomy 19:15).
      b. "... in the mouth of two or three witnesses shall every word may be established" (Matthew 18:16).
      c. "... in the mouth of two or three witnesses shall every word be established" (II Corinthians 13:1).

      d. "Two are better than one ... and a threefold cord is not easily broken" (Ecclesiastes 4:9,12).
4. God has provided a threefold witness to establish believers:
      a. "For there are three that bear record in heaven, the Father, The Word ("Son" - John 1:1,14), and the Holy Ghost; and these three are one. And there are three that bear witness in earth, the Spirit, and the water, and the blood: and these three agree in one ... He that believeth on the Son of God hath the witness in himself (witness of Blood, Water, Spirit) ..." (I John 5:7-10).

Notice how the threefold pattern emerges:

I JOHN 5:8	JOHN 3:3&5	ACTS 2:38
Witness of Blood	Born Again	Repent
Witness of Water	Born of Water	Be Baptized
Witness of Spirit	Born of Spirit	Receive Gifts of Holy Ghost

5. The threefold witness of blood, water, and spirit is found in Israel's deliverance from Egyptian bondage. The Passover lamb was killed, and its blood applied to the

Israelite's dwelling place. The last tentacles of Egyptian bondage were destroyed as Israel passed through the Red Sea, and the pursuing armies of Egypt were buried in that same water. The law was given on Mt. Sinai at

Pentecost: at a later Pentecost, after God's perfect and final Passover "Lamb" was slain at Calvary, the Holy Ghost was given to do what the law could not do in God's people (Acts 1:8). When we repent and turn to Jesus, and His blood is applied to our lives, we are free from the specter of death. We have entered into eternal life.

But to be established in God, we must make a clear break with our past. Further, to be able to function as a Christian and a witness to our Lord Jesus Christ, we must have the power from high - to be baptized with the Holy Ghost (Matthew 5:11; John 7:37-39; Acts 1:4-8; 2:37,38).

4. CAN A PERSON BE SAVED WITHOUT WATER BAPTISM AND WITH THE HOLY GHOST?

1. Yes, but establishment in God requires a believer to "observe all things whatsoever I have commanded you" (Matthew 28:20). Biblical accounts of believers who were saved without being established through baptism experiences are exceptional.
    a. For example, the thief on the cross didn't have a chance to go beyond salvation (Luke 23:39-43) but clearly repented unto salvation.

2. Those who hear truth and fail to act on it soon fall into deception (James 1:22) and disobedience, which is sin. (James 4:17) For them, backsliding is inevitable, and they are worse off than before (II Peter 2:21).

5. HOW TO BE A WITNESS FOR JESUS (THE PRACTICAL SIDE).

1. Remember that a witness is something you are rather than something you say or do (Acts 1:8).

2. Ensure you are "walking the walk" before attempting to "talk the talk."

3. The objective of personal evangelism is to bring a sinner to repentance and get him established in God.
    a. Requires a change of heart (II Corinthians 5:17).
    b. Lead him to full commitment:
        i. Present Jesus as Lord, not just Savior (Romans 10:9; Philippians 2:9-11).
        ii. Simply mouthing the "sinner's prayer" without genuine repentance is a sham.
    c. Water Baptism and Baptism with the Holy Ghost should follow as soon as possible! Follow the pattern of a threefold conversion experience.

4. Remember, you can't save anybody - that's God's job; we simply share the truth and let God do the rest. Not everybody will respond immediately.
    a. "No man can come to me, except the Father which hath sent me draw him" (John 6:44).
    b. "And I, if I be lifted up from earth, will draw all men unto me" (John 12:32).
    c. "I have planted, Apollos watered; but God giveth the increase" (I Corinthians 3:6).
    d. "So shall my Word be that goeth forth out of my mouth: it shall not return unto me void, but it shall accomplish that which I please, and it shall prosper in the things whereto I sent it" (Isaiah 55:11).

5. Consider your appearance, approach, and attitudes:
    a. Be a good listener. (Both the inquirer and the Holy Ghost).
    b. Immodest/eccentric clothing can be distracting or repelling.
    c. Be conscious of personal hygiene. (Unclean clothes, hands, bad breath, and body odor).
    d. Be gentle. (No hustling or "sales" techniques).
    e. Share only what you know for sure - all else is lifeless information.
        i. "But to continue thou in the things which thou has learned and hast been assured of knowing of whom thou has learned them" (II Timothy 3:14).
        ii. Don't misquote or guess at the scriptures!
        iii. A brief word of relevant testimony can be helpful (Revelations 12:11).
    f. Exude confidence:
        i. It's contagious and releases faith.
        ii. You are an "agent" - God's responsible for the result.
        iii. Proverbs 3:5,6.
        iv. Galatians 2:20.
        v. Impart peace, not anxiety.
    g. Keep it simple. Meet a person at his point of need and minister from that point.
        i. Share scriptural principles in plain language. A sinner has little capacity for yards of scripture in 17th-century English.
        ii. Read actual scripture verses sparingly.
        iii. A canned checklist is more harmful than good.
    h. Always be prepared and equipped to share Jesus:
        i. II Timothy 2:15.
        ii. II Timothy 4:2.

6. If you are unsure of yourself, ask a more experienced saint to disciple you in soul-winning (follow an altar worker; listen and back him with prayer as he ministers - until you learn the ropes).

PERSONAL WITNESS
PART 2

"And when Simon (a recently converted sorcerer) saw that through laying on of the apostles' hands the Holy Ghost was given, he offered them money, saying, give me also this power that on whomever I lay hands, he may receive the Holy Ghost" (Acts 8:18,19). And, inexplicably, the mystery continues among saints today - Spirit-filled saints who can skillfully and scripturally explain the Baptism in the Holy Ghost and quickly lead an inquiring believer into this wonderful and necessary experience in God (II Corinthians 3:6). This class embraces both the scriptural and the practical reality of ministering the Baptism of the Holy Ghost.

1. **SCRIPTURAL BASIS.**

    1. Repent, be baptized, and receive the gift of the Holy Ghost (threefold conversion experience) (Acts 2:38).

    2. Baptism with the Holy Ghost is a separate experience which follows salvation:
        a. Examine the timeline from Passover to Pentecost (50 days).
            i. Jesus to Peter at Passover supper: "... when thou art converted" (Luke 22:32).
            ii. Jesus to disciples when He first appears to them after the resurrection, "... receive ye the Holy Ghost" (Passover plus 3 days) (John 20:19-22).
            iii. Ascension Day on Mount of Olives (Passover plus 4 days) (Acts 1:3-5,8).
            iv. They waited and prayed as Jesus had instructed (Acts 1:12,14).

  v. The day of Pentecost is fully come (Passover plus 50 days) (Acts 2:1).

3. The experience and its manifestations.
   a. This part was a singular experience, not repeated in scripture (Acts 2:2,3).
      i. Sound "... as a rushing, mighty wind" (Verse 2).
      ii. "Appeared unto them cloven tongues, like as of fire and it sat upon each of them" (Verse 3).
      iii. Jesus' baptism was also singular: The Holy Ghost descended in bodily shape like a dove ..., and a voice came from Heaven... "Thou art my beloved son ..." (Luke 3:21,22).
   b. "(They) began to speak with other tongues, as the Spirit gave them utterance" (Acts 2:4).
   c. Visible/Audible evidence of Holy Spirit Baptism:
      i. Initial Pentecost experience (Acts 2:4-11).
      ii. Believers at Samaria (Acts 8:14-19).
      iii. Gentiles of Cornelius' household (Acts 10:44-48).
      iv. Disciples at Ephesus (Acts 19:1-6).

4. Detractors, then and now.
   a. "It's a dangerous and unseemly display of emotionalism"- or "These men are full of new wine."
   b. "It was for the Apostolic Age, but not for now."
      i. Joel's prophesy (Joel 2:28-32) is still being fulfilled (Acts 2:16-21).
      ii. Spirit to be poured out on all flesh (Verse 17).
      iii. There is to be a great upheaval of nature - "before the great and notable (Joel said

            "terrible") day of the Lords' coming (Verse 19:20).
- iv. Did "whosoever shall call on the name of the Lord shall be saved: also pass into extinction with the "Apostolic Age?" (Verse 21).
- v. The promise is to - You: your children; all who are afar off; as many as the Lord shall call (Acts 2:38,39)
- vi. What is the "Apostolic Age?" Apostles still ministering to the church today! (Ephesians 4:11-13).

5. Misunderstanding concerning "Tongues".
    a. I Corinthians 12:10, 28-30, deals with the "operation of the gift of tongues in the assembly."
        - i. The entire twelfth chapter speaks of the Body's (Church's) functioning in reference to the operations of gifts.
        - ii. Ministry gifts (from Apostolic ministry to operations of tongues) are set in the church (Verse 28).
        - iii. Verses 10 and 28 speak of "divers" or "diversities" (different but recognizable as human languages) of tongues.
        - iv. Uninterrupted ("unknown") tongues are for one own personal benefit.
        - v. Notice the difference in usage between "unknown" tongues here and "divers" kinds of tongues in Chapter 12.
        - vi. Spoken to God, not to men (Verse 2).
        - vii. Speaking mysteries in the spirit (Verse 2).
        - viii. Prophecy benefits others (Verse 3).
        - ix. Tongues + interpretation + prophecy = benefits the assembled church (Verse 5).

            x. Speaking in "unknown" tongues benefits only the speaker (Verse 4).
    b. An "unknown" tongue doesn't require specific mental understanding (I Corinthians 14:13-19).
            i. It is a spiritual expression in prayer or song (Verses 14,15).
            ii. It is a legitimate expression of personal worship (Verse 15).
            iii. It is solely for personal edification - others receive nothing without interpretation (Verse 17).
            iv. To benefit the assembly, tongues and interpretation with straight prophecy or preaching is more desirable than hearing an "unknown" tongue (Verses 18,19).
            v. Paul worshiped (prayed and\or sang) in tongues a great deal during his private devotion (Verse 18,19).
    c. I Corinthians 14:26-33 speaks of order in the operation of tongues in the assembly:
            i. All things are done unto edifying (Verse 26).
            ii. Unknown: tongues are spoken aloud, for the assembly to hear, requires interpretation (Verses 27,28).
            iii. Private prayer\worship in tongues is permissible in the assembly if kept under control and in order (Verses 28,32,33).
            iv. Spoken quietly to self and to God, not causing confusion or offense.
            v. The speaker is in control of himself.
            vi. Don't forbid tongues! "Let all things be done ... (do them) decently and in order" (I Corinthians 14:39-40).
            vii. Praying in the Spirit (tongues) builds faith (Jude 20).

2. PRACTICAL MINISTRY - BAPTISM WITH THE HOLY SPIRIT.

1. Be confident in the Lord; you can impart to and release faith in the inquirer.

2. Determine where he is with God (he may not be saved or have unconfessed sin to deal with).

3. Give him minimum adequate instruction to prepare him to receive Baptism.
    a. Ensure understanding without overloading with extraneous information.
    b. Brief him on the mechanics:
        i. Tell what to expect, then do it.
        ii. Put him at ease:
        iii. Relax: nothing spooky or strenuous involved.
        iv. "God desires it for you more than you desire it for yourself."
        v. Physical position is not crucial (standing, sitting, kneeling, etc.).

4. Mechanics:
    a. Pray first.
        i. Tune self.
        ii. Stir candidates' faith.
        iii. Listen to the candidate and God.
    b. Cleansing period - updates sanctification (confession, preparation of vessel).
    c. Prayer and prayer of affirmation aloud (it stirs faith).
    d. Have the inquirer ask Jesus to baptize him with the Holy Ghost.
    e. Lay on hands - pray in tongues.

f. Encourage him to open his mouth and speak as the spirit gives him utterance.

REMEMBER YOU CAN'T BAPTIZE HIM; JESUS DOES!!!

5. Problems
   a. Usually caused by a lack of operative faith.
   b. Some won't exercise requisite faith at the moment.
      i. Pray that the Lord would release an expression of the Spirit.
      ii. Encourage him: God still loves\has not rejected him.
      iii. Suggest that he get alone with God and simply begin to try speaking in tongues (this often helps shy/timid people).

6. Afterward
   a. Encourage him to exercise his "prayer language" (I Corinthians 14:14,15; Jude 20).
   b. Warn of the enemy's attempts to lie and rob him of the experience!

If you require any further information on any of the classes in this booklet, please contact the Covenant Life International office at 865-494-5144 or **www.cl.life**

ABOUT THE AUTHOR

Bishop Tony McAfee's passion for spreading the message of hope and restoration goes beyond his role as the founder and Lead Pastor of Covenant Life International. He has dedicated his life to serving others as teacher, life coach, and community leader, even outside the walls of the Church. In addition to his duties at the Church, Tony also serves as a Chaplain for the Knox County Sheriff's Department. He brings comfort and support to those facing difficult and devastating times, showing his true heart of compassion and empathy. As a dedicated board member, Tony has been a pivotal board member in the Philip Cameron Ministries and Orphans Hands, significantly contributing to its impactful work of rescuing young children from sex trafficking.

Together with his wife, Pastor Cyndi, they continue to build a legacy that extends beyond their own family. Their two daughters have followed in their footsteps and are serving full-time in the ministry. This is a testament to the firm foundation of faith and love that Tony and Cyndi have instilled in their family. They also prioritize spending quality time with their daughters, sons-in-law, and grandchildren, cherishing every moment together. Their dedication to their family and community is truly inspiring and a reflection of their unwavering faith and love for God.

The impact of Bishop Tony McAfee's teachings and ministry extends far beyond the U.S. and South America, where he has traveled extensively. His message of hope and restoration has touched the lives of countless individuals and continues to do so through his work at Covenant Life International. With over 30 years of experience as a Lead Pastor, his wisdom and guidance have brought light and clarity to those seeking spiritual guidance. His selfless service and dedication to spreading love and hope have genuinely made a difference in the world.

Has Grounded & Growing propelled your spiritual growth? Pastor Tony's debut work, "Divine Interruptions," offers profound solace if you've wrestled with the agonizing questions: Where is God amidst life's devastating storms? Where is He when your trials eclipse all others? This inspirational exploration of Job's life provides invaluable guidance for those moments when your most profound questions seem unanswerable, offering comfort and wisdom during your darkest hours.

Contact Covenant Life Church for details of how to get copies of Bishop Tony McAfee's books. **Phone: (865)494-5144**

www.bishoptonymcafee.com

Made in the USA
Middletown, DE
08 February 2025